DIC PENDERYN

THE MAN AND THE MARTYR

'When two or three were killed at Manchester, it was called the *Peterloo massacre* and the newspapers for weeks wrote it up as the most outrageous and wicked proceeding ever heard of... this Welsh riot is scarcely mentioned.' – HARRIET ARBUTHNOT, POLITICAL DIARIST & MISTRESS OF THE DUKE OF WELLINGTON, WRITING IN 1831

'In Merthyr Tydfil in 1831, the prehistory of the Welsh working class comes to an end. Its history begins.' – GWYN ALF WILLIAMS, HISTORIAN

'[Dic Penderyn] is now an important cult figure in the working-class struggle... one small burning flame of Merthyr's fiery legacy.' – GARETH E REES, AUTHOR

'The young miner became a symbol for those who tried to fight and resist oppression, wherever it was to be found. He became a working class hero, a folk hero, who has remained in the minds and the affections of all Welsh people... remembered as a true Welsh martyr.' – PHIL CARRADICE, AUTHOR

'The Merthyr Rising and Dic Penderyn deserve their place alongside the Tolpuddle Martyrs... the revolutionary Russian workers and all the other class fighters who risked life and limb in the fight for a decent existence.' – JOE ATTARD, *SOCIALIST APPEAL*

'Penderyn was the victim of a grave miscarriage of justice... The fact that this injustice took place nearly 200 years ago does not make it any less important.' – STEPHEN KINNOCK, MP

DIC PENDERYN

THE MAN AND THE MARTYR

SALLY ROBERTS JONES

Acknowledgements

Every researcher knows how much they owe to fellow workers in the field and I acknowledge with much pleasure that help over the four decades of my research. I would also like to thank Y Lolfa and its staff – in particular Carolyn, my editor – for their work in bringing Dic's story so effectively into print.

First impression: 2022

The publishers wish to acknowledge the support of the Books Council of Wales.

Cover design: Tanwen Haf
Cover image: Pearson Scott Foresman

ISBN: 978 1 80099 184 2

Published and printed in Wales
on paper from well-maintained forests by
Y Lolfa Cyf., Talybont, Ceredigion SY24 5HE
website www.ylolfa.com
e-mail ylolfa@ylolfa.com
tel 01970 832 304

Contents

Preface   7

Introduction   8

Chapter 1: Early Years   13

Chapter 2: Over to Merthyr   25

Chapter 3: Riots and Risings   42

Chapter 4: The Trial   59

Chapter 5: Last Days   80

Chapter 6: Aftermath   101

Chapter 7: Afterlife   125

Appendices   145

  i Accounts of the Execution: 145

    a) Biography of Revd David Williams   145

    b) Biography of Revd Edmund Evans   147

  ii Account of the Funeral   150

  iii Letters to the Press: 156

    a) account of meeting the man who stabbed the soldier   156

    b) Isaac Evans's letter   158

  iv Lewis Davies, *Ystoriau Siluria*   162

  v Dic's Last Letter   165

Endnotes   168

Picture Section   175

Bibliography   182

Index   186

But still we hold in honour
The men who struck and bled
For freedom and for justice
And to give our people bread.
And the time is surely coming
When Wales must more show
The courage of Penderyn
So many years ago.

– from *The Merthyr Rising* by Harri Webb

Preface

THE PRESENT ACCOUNT has been several decades in the making and I owe thanks to many people for information and ideas. Most of all, however, I owe thanks to Steffan ap Dafydd, fellow enthusiast and researcher. Steffan's particular interest was Lewsyn yr Heliwr and the other men who were also transported to Australia after the Rising. He was working in parallel on an account of these, and we shared our research and our findings over the years. Although we did not always agree on the results, we always agreed to differ. I owe Steffan a particular debt because although much of the material was available locally, I was not able to visit the National Archives, which hold many of the official trial documents, and Steffan generously gave me access to his own research there.

Steffan died suddenly, without warning, early in 2020, before his work was completed. A year or so before that he had become a local councillor and been able to put his principles into practice, helping to build a better world. This book is therefore dedicated to him and to all those who work for social justice and equality.

Sally Roberts Jones
July 2022

Introduction

AT EIGHT O'CLOCK on the morning of Saturday, 13 August 1831, Richard Lewis was hanged outside Cardiff Gaol for his part in what the authorities called the Merthyr Riots of May and June of the same year. In the late afternoon of Sunday, 14 August he was buried in St Mary's churchyard, Aberafan. These are almost the only undisputed facts in the record of his life, and even these have a kind of ambiguity. Meanwhile, Richard Lewis has vanished, giving place to the legendary Dic Penderyn: first martyr of the workers' cause in Wales. What follows is an attempt to discover at least something of what lies behind the legend and – if possible – why Richard Lewis, among all those who were executed, transported or imprisoned in the search for social justice, should be so well remembered, and even honoured.

Richard Lewis and his family were not ironmasters or squires, or even shopkeepers, whose possessions or trades gave them authority and a place in the history of the community. The Lewises belonged to the little people, those who appear on the margins of history: ironworkers, miners, labourers, servant girls – the men and women without whom civilisation could not exist, but who live and die, even today, for the most part nameless and forgotten. This, of course, presents the biographer with a problem. In Dic's case, he stood in the full glare of public interest for perhaps the last four or five weeks of his life – at the time of his trial and the fight for a reprieve – but there are almost no documented details of the 23 years before that, or of his family and their response to the events of that summer of anguish. And yet, though the sources are so few and so elusive, once investigated thoroughly, they slowly begin to build into a remarkably solid picture of the young miner who was hanged on that wet, grey Saturday morning in August 1831.

In what follows, I have tried to show how the picture was assembled. It might be useful here to note some of the pieces that make up the picture: the sources from which this biography has been written. The information they provide is patchy and always has to be handled with care, but it is surprisingly consistent. There is a tendency these days to assume that oral tradition – anything not written down – is too unreliable to be considered seriously, which would mean that much of what we have been told about Dic's earlier life and his character would have to be discounted. However, experience demonstrates the fallacy here: documents and traditions *both* have to be treated with caution.

The first and most detailed sources are, of course, the contemporary reports of the trial and execution in the various documents and letters sent to the Home Secretary and other members of the government, together with the accounts in *The Cambrian* newspaper. At one point it was thought that much of this documentation was no longer available, but recent research has uncovered most, if not yet all, of this material. (Substantial portions of the official documents are available in print, for instance in Gwyn A Williams's detailed account, *The Merthyr Rising*, and in the Author's Note to Alexander Cordell's novel *The Fire People*.) Normally one might have expected this to be the end of the matter, as it was for earlier would-be rebels, but if Dic Penderyn was dead, he was certainly not forgotten. In 1865 and 1870 the magazine *Eurgrawn Wesleyaidd* (The Wesleyan Treasury) printed articles on two of the ministers who accompanied Dic to the scaffold, and though they did not highlight the execution, both articles included reminiscences of the event. Then in 1874, 43 years after Dic's death, the *Western*

Mail carried a report that a minister travelling in America had heard the deathbed confession of the man who had really committed the crime for which Dic died. This was followed in 1884 by letters in *Tarian y Gweithiwr* (The Worker's Shield), one of which was from Isaac Evans, nephew of the man who married Dic's widow. Isaac reported what his uncle had told him of the events in Merthyr and Dic's capture.

Another reminiscence appeared in 1919 in *Y Drysorfa* (The Treasury), this time the memories of an old man (over 80 when he told his story *c.*1900) who had been present as a child at the execution and followed the coffin to Aberafan. Two years later, in 1921, Lewis Davies included the story of Dic Penderyn in his book of historical tales for children, *Ystoriau Siluria*, and in 1928 D Emrys Lewis contributed an article on 'A Forgotten Martyr' to the *Transactions* of the Aberafan and Margam Historical Society, and another one – telling much the same story, but with other added details – to the *Welsh Outlook*. Then in 1933 an exchange of letters in the *Western Mail* included a memoir by James Evans, Dic's great-nephew, who wrote to the same paper again in 1947, just after a play on Dic's life had been broadcast on the radio. James Evans was elderly by then – almost 80 in 1947. In 1945 Islwyn ap Nicholas produced a short biography of 'the Welsh Rebel and Martyr', followed in 1956 by Harri Webb's pamphlet, *Dic Penderyn and the Merthyr Rising of 1831*. In 1966 local trade unionists placed a memorial on Dic's grave in St Mary's churchyard. More recently, plaques have been placed on the entrance to the market in Cardiff, once the site of Cardiff Gaol, and on the Central Library in Merthyr Tydfil. Sadly, the Cardiff market plaque has had to be corrected at least once.

All of these are printed sources, but their origins vary. The court records relating to the last part of Dic's life are official and the information they contain is therefore seen as acceptable. There are, as has been said, no such official records of the earlier years of his life, but there is a strong body of tradition about them – especially as regards his youth in Aberafan – which also came to be recorded in print. The earliest of these is Lewis Davies's *Ystoriau Siluria* (1921), and it is curious in that Davies accepts Dic's guilt and therefore paints him as an odd mixture of the heroic and the villainous. Later Islwyn ap Nicholas's biography (1945) and Harri Webb's booklet (1956) were apparently drawn from local tradition alone, but they are consistent and where the details can be checked, they hold up. For example, Islwyn ap Nicholas says that Dic's younger siblings were present at the execution. Originally this seemed to be an invented detail, but we now know that in addition to the officially recorded John and Elizabeth, Dic did have two other (probably younger) siblings, Matthew and Sarah. Islwyn ap Nicholas was not sure of the names and calls them Thomas and Rachel, but they did exist. We do know that local historians like Martin Phillips and A Leslie Evans collected information and traditions about Dic and Islwyn ap Nicholas acknowledged Phillips's help – he is the most likely source for Davies too. There is an obvious difference between these accounts and those traditions (like no grass growing on his grave) which are clearly drawn from folklore. If it seems surprising that such a detailed tradition existed, one should remember that Dic was only 23 when he was executed, and he had left Aberafan for Merthyr only 11 years before that. There would have been plenty of friends and family around who would have known and remembered him and passed the story on. Gwyn A Williams, author of the fullest account of the Merthyr Rising and himself a Merthyr boy, bears witness to this, commenting on how often family conversations 'curled back to 1831'.

All of these are in one way or another non-fiction accounts of Richard Lewis's life and times, but over the years his story has also inspired novels, plays and poems and these too are part of the legend. They deserve to be considered, partly as testimony to the way in which Dic's story has survived and captured the imagination of each of the generations that have followed, but also because they can at times add a further dimension to their hero.

This is not an account of the Merthyr Rising as such – others, most notably Gwyn A Williams and David Jones, have already written detailed and distinguished histories of the events there in 1831. Instead, this is an account of the life of Richard Lewis insofar as we can know it, and of the world in which he lived.

CHAPTER 1

Early Years

RICHARD LEWIS – LATER to be known as 'Dic Penderyn' – was born in about the year 1808, in a small cottage known as 'Penderyn' in the parish of Aberafan in the west of Glamorgan. His father was Lewis Lewis, a miner; of his mother nothing is known except for her name: Mary, née Jenkins. This is the most likely summary of Dic's origins, but even this is not undisputed. It may have been the anonymous 80 year old reported in *Y Drysorfa*[1] who first linked the Lewises with Pyle in print, saying that they lived in 'a little place called Penderyn, in Pyle'. He did not say that Dic was born there, but he did go on to speak of Dic's brother John, a lime-burner by trade, who worked in the Pyle and Cefn Cribwr area for some years. John Lewis's daughter, identified only as 'Miss Lewis', later lived at Kenfig Hill (which borders Pyle), where Dic's great-nephew James Evans remembered visiting her,[2] and Dic's brother-in-law Morgan Howells also wrote about visiting the family in the area in the late 1840s[3] – John Lewis would, of course, also have been Howells's brother-in-law.

Possibly the 80 year old, speaking many years later and knowing of the connection between John's family and Pyle, assumed that Lewis Lewis (John and Dic's father) had also lived in the village, and so placed Penderyn cottage there and not at Aberafan. As it happened, there *was* a Lewis family living in the area, at Cornelly, at the relevant time: the parents were

Lewis and Mary Lewis and the baptisms of their children are recorded in the Kenfig parish registers from 1807 onwards.[4] However, this Lewis Lewis was a shoemaker, not a miner, as Dic's father was said to have been, and his daughter Mary was baptised at Kenfig in February 1821, two to three years after Dic's family is said to have moved to Merthyr. Bearing in mind also that Dic's known sister Elizabeth was born in 1800 and there is no mention anywhere of a sister Mary, it does not seem likely that these Lewises were Dic's immediate kin.

The current interest in family history lies behind more recent suggestions concerning the Lewis family. One gave Dic a sizeable family of descendants in the Rhondda, but further research showed these to be from his widow's second marriage.[5] Another has tried to link the Lewises with some of Aberafan's leading families,[6] but Welsh genealogy is notoriously complicated by the limited number of names used – hence the need for nicknames. Another family tradition linked the Lewis family originally to Llanfair-ar-y-Bryn, Carmarthenshire.[7]

It was Pamela Lewis, a descendant of Dic's brother John, who told me that Dic's mother's maiden name had been Mary Jenkins. I met Miss Lewis, a teacher, twice at the annual commemorations organised in Cardiff in the 2000s by local councillor Charlie Gale, and she told me that the family had continued to have a strong socialist tradition – one that she endorsed herself.

Neither Dic nor any other potential Lewis offspring appear in the parish registers of St Mary's, Aberafan, but in that period, before births, marriages and deaths had to be officially registered from 1836 onwards, non-appearance could have had a number of explanations – even just a vicar who did not keep up his records. Perhaps more relevantly, the Lewises were Nonconformists, so if there ever was a record, it might well have been in a chapel register rather than that belonging to the parish, but the surviving records of the most likely connection, the group of Calvinistic Methodists that met at Dyffryn Barn, do not begin until later. Certainly Aberafan was usually described as Dic's 'native place' and he was buried there. If the much-damaged stone on his grave does refer to him, it describes him as 'of this Town', and in 1831 Lord Bute, writing about the aftermath of the trial, seems to have had no doubt that Richard Lewis came from Aberafan. All of these points would seem to support the statement that Penderyn cottage was at Aberafan, not at Pyle. Although 'long since demolished' even in 1944, the cottage apparently stood in Penrhiw at the bottom of Cwmafan Road, where the M4 motorway now crosses it.[8] An article in the *Glamorgan Gazette* on 17 March 1933 says that 'some remains' of the cottage may still be seen. This was on the authority of Mr John Lane, formerly of Cwmafan, whose memory would have gone back to the late 1860s. The number of local traditions about Dic's childhood are also strong pointers to an origin in Aberafan.

On the other hand, one does have to account for the nickname 'Penderyn', both as applied to the cottage and to Dic himself. Since we do not know when he acquired this nickname, it is possible that it came from the later period when he was working in the Penderyn area, but it is generally associated with his birthplace in Aberafan. One or two sources – among them the late trade union leader Clive Jenkins – suggest that 'Dic Penderyn' is a corruption of 'Dic fel Deryn': 'Dic like a bird'. Clive Jenkins, himself from the Aberafan district, says he was told this in school, but even if this was a genuine tradition, reflecting the fact that the young boy was light-hearted – 'free as a bird' – or that he often whistled, the Welsh usage would surely have been 'Dic Deryn', like the character in the Welsh-language soap opera *Pobol y Cwm*.[9] Then again, why was the cottage called Penderyn? Farms had names, and the occasional cottage might be named for some particular feature it possessed, like Twll yn y Wal in Margam, which had an upper window through which to feed the outside passengers in stage coaches, but this was unusual. And why should Dic, either then or in later years in Merthyr, also be known as 'Penderyn'? Welsh nicknames serve a very practical purpose of identification, of distinguishing one John Jones or Bill Williams or Bob Owen from all the others, and it is difficult to see why a cottage in Aberafan should act as a reference point in distant Merthyr – 'Dic Aberafan', perhaps, but not 'Dic Penderyn', unless Penderyn had a wider relevance.

It is, though, possible to speculate – though it cannot be more than speculation – that Lewis Lewis, Dic's father, originally came from the village or area of Penderyn on the Glamorgan-Breconshire border, and came down to Aberafan to look for work either in the newly-opened mines in Cwm Bychan or Cwm Brombil or in the expanding ironworks at the Afan Forge. He might have come via Pyle, where John Bedford's ironworks were in operation in the 1790s and there was work for an ironstone miner. Some such journey would explain several later mysteries – in particular Dic's link with the other Lewis Lewis, 'Lewsyn yr Heliwr', who did come from Penderyn and might in this case have been a very distant cousin, too distant to be fully recognised, but a 'connection' rather than a friend. And if Dic's father, once arrived in Aberafan, met and married a local girl, perhaps from one of the ruling burgess families of Aberafan, it would explain why her son was remembered and honoured in that town when even Merthyr, officially at least, had forgotten him. The Jenkinses were certainly one of the old families of the town, and even today, with a population of many thousands, the old kinship links are still important.[10] As for the name Penderyn, that would then commemorate both the family's cottage and the paternal village, a logical choice for a nickname used in Merthyr.

Richard Lewis spent his first 11 years – almost half his life – in Aberafan and the influences that he met with there were to have a permanent importance for him. Aberafan in 1808 was still not much more than a village, with a population of just over 300, but it also had a civic tradition going back several hundred years to the later Middle Ages, something which gave the town an unusual degree of independence. Although the Talbot family of Margam and Penrice, and the Earl of Jersey – whose Briton Ferry estate included much of Cwmafan – each had considerable influence locally, Aberafan itself was not dominated by any great family.

The town was a huddle of mostly single-storey thatched cottages, presided over by St Mary's Church and the ruins of the ancient castle of the Lords of Afan on its mound next to the church. It was still pre-industrial: mines were being opened just up the valley and a succession of entrepreneurs were attempting to start up or expand a local iron industry, but the nearest serious industrial complex was that of the English Copper Company at Taibach, two miles away. The great event of each year was the installation of the new Portreeve (mayor) of the borough on the castle mound. Travellers almost invariably described Aberafan as a 'dirty little village', or words to that effect – possibly because copper slag was used to surface the roads in the area, with resulting dust.

Edward Donovan, who stayed at the Globe Hotel on the High Street in 1804, some four years before Dic was born,[11] described how he was kept awake by the village blacksmith, who first fought everyone in sight inside the inn, and then stood outside in the street at midnight, singing extempore verses in Welsh and swearing vengeance on his enemies. It was a typical Welsh market town: small, close-knit and unsophisticated, but very much alive.

'Penderyn' would have been one of the single-storey thatched cottages, shining outside from the annual coat of limewash so typical of Glamorgan, but dark and probably damp inside. We do not know exactly how many people it had to house – Lewis Lewis and his wife Mary, of course; their daughter Elizabeth, born c.1800; Dic himself; John the lime-burner of Pyle; and Matthew. James Evans, Dic's great-nephew, spoke of another girl: Sarah. These names are attested by the family. Later writers such as Islwyn ap Nicholas give others – Thomas for Dic's brother, Mary, Gwen or Rachel for his sister, Mari Howells or Sun Heron for his wife, but these are simply guesswork.

By all accounts, Dic himself was full of life and vigour, and even at an early age a leader among his fellows. Two stories in particular are told of his childhood in Aberafan, probably dating from c.1817, when he was about nine or ten years of age. The first[12] tells how Dic and his friend Wil, son of the local blacksmith, were scrumping apples in a neighbour's orchard when the neighbour appeared and gave chase. The boys got away, but Dic had been recognised and the next day the owner of the orchard called at Dic's home, accompanied by the schoolmaster. Dic was questioned, but no amount of threats could make him betray his friend, not even the sound beating that followed. (One wonders if young Wil was the son of the poetic blacksmith who 'entertained' Donovan when he passed through Aberafan in 1804.)

At that date the River Afan still followed its original course, flowing through the town and then looping south-eastwards to join the River Ffrwdwyllt and meet the sea at the old Bar of Afan at Taibach. The old harbour had always carried on a busy shipping trade, first in the wool exported by the monks of Margam Abbey, and then, by Dic's time, in the output of the copper works and the local mines. It was a lively place and must have been an ideal playground for the more adventurous local boys, of whom Dic was one. Perhaps he heard his first English there, from one of the sailors or one of the West Country men who came across the Bristol Channel to find work. Aberafan itself was solidly Welsh-speaking.

One day Dic and another friend, Dafi Cound, were playing about next to the harbour wall when, in the course of a scuffle, Dafi fell into the harbour.[13] Normally this would have meant no more than a wetting, and no doubt a scolding when Dafi got home, but this time he fell on a protruding beam and was knocked unconscious. Dic dived into the water at once and got his friend ashore, but though Dafi was saved, he had broken his back in the fall and was crippled for life.

Although both stories show Dic in a favourable light as a brave, quick-witted and loyal friend, there are elements of realism in both – the apple-stealing and the broken back – which suggest that the stories are genuine and not simply the kind of folk tale that gathers round any hero. (Islwyn ap Nicholas tells them most fully, but the story about Dafi Cound first appears in Lewis Davies's *Ystoriau Siluria* in 1921 – both evidently drew on local sources.) The Cound family still live in the area and in the early 1800s had close connections with the local Calvinistic Methodists. Much later, at the time of the 1851 census, Dic's brother-in-law Morgan Howells was staying with the Counds in Taibach.

As has been said, we know almost nothing about Dic's parents. Lewis Davies suggests that Dic's mother died when he was very young and it was his sister Elizabeth who acted as mother to the younger children,[14] but this may simply be an assumption drawn from the fact that we hear nothing about her. On the other hand, if true, it would explain why it was Elizabeth to whom Dic wrote before his execution, to arrange for his body to be taken back to Aberafan. Dic's father also vanishes very early on from what little record there is, and we do not even know if he was still alive in 1831 at the time of the riots. Things that the sources do agree on, however, are that Dic came from a respectable, hard-working family, and that his parents were God-fearing people whose family life was centred round the Methodist chapel. This was presumably the Calvinistic Methodist cause; though they had individual members in the town earlier, the Wesleyan Methodists did not establish themselves in Aberafan as a church until some years later. Also, Dic's sister Elizabeth was a member with the Calvinistic Methodists at Newport when she married Morgan Howells, their minister, and in the context, this is a further strong indication of the family's allegiance.

Nowadays there is a tendency to view this branch of Methodism through the distorting mirror of late Victorian and Edwardian attitudes, and so to perceive it (often quite unfairly) as narrow, exclusive, concerned more with social propriety and maintaining the status quo than with either spiritual growth or social reform – not something one would expect to find congenial to Wales's first labour martyr. Yet whatever the rights or wrongs of this picture, it is a long way from the fellowship in which the young Richard Lewis grew up and which helped to form his habits and beliefs.

At the beginning of the nineteenth century, Calvinistic Methodism was still very close to the passionate commitment of its founding fathers – men like William Williams Pantycelyn, hymnwriter, tea merchant and prodigious traveller; or Howell Harris, who combined his spiritual duties with an interest in improving agriculture and developing new forms of communal living. Certainly their eyes were firmly fixed on heaven, but their feet were equally firmly fixed on earth, and marriage guidance was as valid a subject for discussion as the glory of God. There was an element of puritanism in their belief, and a feeling of separation from the world and its temptations, but it was usually something positive, not a mere denial for denial's sake, as it later tended to become. For instance, there was a young man, Thomas Robert from Taibach, who was a skilful player of bando (a form of hockey, usually played between parish teams). He was the Barry John or Gareth Edwards of his day, dedicated to the game, strict in his training and using his slight build to beat his bulkier opponents.[15] Then, in 1806, he was converted and decided to give up the frivolous pursuit of bando – though not without many regrets. Naturally his teammates and their supporters tried every possible way to persuade him to play again, even sending him a parcel containing one of the red and white shirts worn by the players, in the hope that 'the very sight of it would break his resistance'. Sadly for the team, even this was not enough and Thomas

Robert ended his life as one of the saintly deacons of Dyffryn Chapel (though he never became teetotal).[16] As a small boy, Dic would have known him by sight, and no doubt heard the saga of the lost champion.

What is perhaps less often acknowledged is the importance of the chapels in providing ordinary working men and women with an opportunity to learn a wide variety of practical skills. Setting up a chapel was a major operation, involving the raising and management of funds, the organisation of the building work – and often the members provided their own architect – and the running of the chapel once built. On the intellectual side, the chapels had been active from their beginnings in teaching members to read, and the Sunday School classes and associated societies taught them to question and debate. The emphasis was obviously on things religious, but the training could be – and often was – used in more secular contexts. Clive Jenkins, the white-collar union leader, comments on this in his autobiography – as a boy in the 1940s, he was a member of the congregation at Dyffryn, Taibach. And though women would not, in those days, find themselves in the Big Seat alongside the deacons, they played their own part in organising chapel events and maintenance.

The Calvinistic Methodist cause had established itself in the neighbourhood of Aberafan some 60 years before Dic was born and by 1808 its adherents met at Dyffryn Barn in Taibach.[17] Dyffryn acted as the centre for a very wide area – from Aberafan to Pyle – and as the population was growing fairly rapidly, it was decided to build a chapel in Aberafan, to provide for the increase. Carmel Chapel, the first purpose-built chapel locally, was completed in 1810, and designed to hold a congregation of up to 200. As the population of Aberafan at that point was only about 300, it is clear that the new building was intended, like Dyffryn, to serve the area, not just the town. It was still very much part of the parent body, however, and initially deacons from Dyffryn watched over the infant cause in Carmel, while Carmel members often attended services in Dyffryn.

Dic was two years old when Carmel opened, and he and his brothers and sisters would probably have been baptised at Dyffryn, which may explain why they do not appear in the Aberafan parish registers – the local Calvinistic Methodist records do not start till 1815. However, when Carmel opened, the Lewises very probably transferred to the more convenient new chapel, and it would have been Carmel Sunday School at which Dic learned to read. If so, then his teacher was Dafydd Rees, the weaver.[18] Dafydd Rees was a very young man – he was only 32 when he died in 1821 – but he had undergone a particularly traumatic conversion and was regarded as a man of remarkably pure life, even among the convinced. He was also very frail, and it was no doubt his ill health that led to the Sunday School being held in the weaver's house until 1820. We know nothing of Dafydd Rees's intellectual attainments but Patrick Brontë, father of the three Brontë sisters and an author himself, began as a weaver, working at home, before he went to Cambridge. Siencyn Penhydd, the converted farmer who dominated the cause locally in the late eighteenth century, was a decidedly homespun prophet, but Carmel's library included a French New Testament of 1816 and books on such subjects as animal husbandry, which suggests a greater degree of sophistication than Siencyn's country parables.[19] (Among Dafydd Rees's successors in the Sunday School was Edward Howe, grandfather of Sir Geoffrey Howe, who himself remembered from time to time sitting through the long Sunday sermons in Carmel, supported by the traditional bag of boiled sweets from Mrs Perkins, the minister's wife.)[20]

It is easy to imagine Dic and his fellows enduring the weekly ration of Sunday School while they cast longing glances out of the cottage window at the inviting shapes of Mynydd Dinas or Mynydd Emroch; school in any form is not usually the native habitat of young humans. Yet however much they yearned to be outside, splashing in the river or building dens on the hillside, they were still being exposed to the one opportunity of acquiring an education that most of them would ever have. The Methodist Revival was notable for its concern with education. Its founders in Wales had been deeply influenced by the Revd Griffith Jones of Llanddowror in Dyfed, originator of the Circulating Schools movement and the Sunday Schools were the heirs of those mobile short courses. They welcomed all ages, from toddlers up to grey-haired senior citizens, and they concentrated on two things – teaching their pupils to read, and then teaching them to consider and discuss what they read. Ostensibly this was intended to make it possible for members to read their Bibles and to discuss those things necessary for their salvation, but in practice these skills, once acquired, could be used for a great many other purposes too, not least the application of ideas of divine justice to the injustices of the everyday world.

Learning to read was one thing; writing was something else. For us the two things go together, but that was not necessarily the case in earlier centuries. Statistics collected in Swansea in the middle of the nineteenth century suggested that some 75% of the men looking for work in the town could read, but only 50% could write. Although the establishment of works schools locally was generally a little later than this, there *were* schools of various kinds around and it was not impossible for a promising youngster to get an education, unless the need to earn a living interfered. According to tradition, Dic worked on at least one local farm.[21] There were always jobs that children could manage – clearing stones from the fields, weeding, scaring crows and so on (as my father-in-law and my uncle were still doing in the early twentieth century) – work that would contribute to the family budget. However it is also said that Dic's parents, seeing his promise, arranged for him to go to school, learning writing and arithmetic there, and that he spent a year or so there just before the family moved to Merthyr Tydfil in 1819.[22] What kind of school might have been available to him is another matter – 1817 was too early for the industrial schools and the local National school was a later foundation. There is a reference to 'the Aberavon Academy', but whether this was for younger children or was a training centre for Nonconformist ministers, like the one in Llangeinor associated with the Price family, is unknown. In some accounts the schoolmaster is said to have had a club foot,[23] and one wonders if Dic's teacher was in fact Dafydd Rees, who taught the Carmel Sunday School children.

As in most of this traditional narrative, we have no definite evidence for the truth of this story. If it is true, it could perhaps help to at least partly explain why the authorities were later to choose him as their scapegoat and to be so determined on his execution. A champion of workers' rights who could write as well as read was a potential danger, and certainly those who knew Dic were impressed by the breadth of his knowledge and described him as educated. However, the Richard Lewis whom genealogical research suggests was Dic Penderyn could only make his mark on his marriage lines, not sign them. He could, perhaps, have injured his hand at the time. He might have dictated that last letter sent to his sister Elizabeth, but he is also said to have written a hymn in his last few days in prison, and there is also mention of 'his last letter to his wife', which was later printed to raise funds for his widow. Possibly this is a confusion with the letter to his sister, though.

Precisely why the family chose to move to Merthyr Tydfil is unknown, but 1819 was not the most prosperous of years locally. Samuel Fothergill Lettsom had begun work on an ironworks in the lower Afan Valley, but his father-in-law, Sir William Garrow, had withdrawn his support and the venture had, for the moment, collapsed. Lettsom finally closed his works on 1 December 1819, and it was some time in that year that the Lewises are said to have moved to Merthyr Tydfil, the great iron town across the mountains.

CHAPTER 2

Over to Merthyr

THERE IS AN old story about an Irishman and his wife who arrived on Kenfig Sands in 1850 and made their way towards Cwmafan, where the man hoped to get work with the English Copper Company. As they came towards the opening of the valley, they saw the glare of the furnaces and heard the thudding of the machinery, and the woman called out in terror, "Patrick, is it to Hell you're taking us?" Something of the sort may well have been the response of the Lewis family as they came in sight of Merthyr: if Cwmafan seemed like the way to Hell, then to the uninitiated the Lewises' new home must have looked like the Inferno itself.

Until the middle of the eighteenth century, Merthyr was a sparsely populated upland parish at the head of the river valley of the Taff. The parish was some six miles long from north to south and an average of three miles wide.[1] Then in 1765 Anthony Bacon, an English entrepreneur, leased land in the area and shortly afterwards began to build an ironworks there. He was followed by other industrialists, mostly English, of whom the most notable were the Crawshay family, the Homfrays, the Hills and the Guests. By 1819 there were four main ironworks: Cyfarthfa (Crawshays), Plymouth (Hills), Penydarren (originally Homfrays, but by 1830 run by William Forman and William Thompson, whose wife was a Homfray) and Dowlais (Guests). In 1801, when the first Census was taken, it was discovered that Merthyr's population had grown to some 7,000 inhabitants and the town was the largest concentration of population in Wales. From then on it grew steadily, and in 1819 there were some 17,000 people living there, in conditions that were often more like a frontier town in the Wild West than anything else.

Cliffe's *Book of South Wales*[2] gives a vivid description of Merthyr in the earlier part of the nineteenth century. The first edition dates from a little later than the arrival of the Lewises, but the general picture cannot have changed much.

> The scene is strange and impressive in broad day-light, but when viewed at night it is wild beyond conception. Darkness is palpable. The mind aids the reality – gives vastness and sublimity to a picture lighted up by a thousand fires. The vivid glow and roaring of the blast furnaces near at hand – the lurid light of distant works – the clanking of hammers and rolling mills, the confused din of massive machinery – the burning headlands – the coke hearths, now if the night be stormy, bursting into sheets of flame, now wrapt in vast and impenetrable clouds of smoke – the wild figures of the workmen, the actors in this apparently infernal scene – all combine to impress the mind of the spectator very powerfully.

Yet this dramatic portrait gives only a part of the truth. To begin with, Merthyr at this point was an overwhelmingly Welsh town:[3] the bulk of its population was Welsh-speaking, drawn from Glamorgan itself and from west Wales – even as late as 1840 only 9% of the people of Merthyr were non-Welsh. In 1819 the Irish were mostly yet to come and such English inhabitants as there were were usually officials in the ironworks, traders or shopkeepers. Hence Merthyr was not only an industrial centre, but also a cultural capital, and one which operated on more than one level. The country people who flocked into Merthyr in search of a better life brought with them the rural culture of ballads and fairs, the *cwrw*

bach and bid ales (parties to raise funds for those in trouble) –
home-grown charities, but often denounced by preachers like
Siencyn Penhydd back home in Aberafan – boxing, foot-racing,
handball and all the fabric of entertainment and self-help that
had made their lives endurable over the centuries. Most of this
was to be suppressed and finally destroyed as Nonconformity
spread and became institutionalised and 'respectable', its
increasingly prim morality taking over from the older social
sanctions such as the *ceffyl pren* – the ritual humiliation and
mock trial that kept offenders within bounds.

On the other hand, elements of these customs and sanctions
did survive. The ropes that the rioters of 1831 used to draw in
their unwilling fellows were clearly variants of the ropes used
at country weddings to capture the members of the wedding
party and oblige them to pay their dues to the local children.
And the casual violence of the crowd at times of social tumult
had its sanction in the communal certainty that their cause
was righteous, something which justified the most extreme
behaviour and allowed the rebels to force even the most
unwilling onlookers into their ranks.

Beyond this, Merthyr in the 1820s saw an intense interest
in Welsh-language culture. This was partly due to the efforts
of Taliesin Williams, otherwise known as Taliesin ap Iolo –
the son of Iolo Morganwg, stonemason, patriot and creative
writer *par excellence*. *Eisteddfodau* were held regularly, Welsh-
language newspapers and books were published and classes
were held to instruct novice poets in the strict metres of
Welsh-language poetry. And beyond this again were the more
purely intellectual activities of the local Unitarians and their
associates – activities which were also politically radical. The
Unitarians were united by more than a common religious
belief, since they were closely connected by marriage and by
commercial links. Their leaders were men of some standing in
local society, well off financially, with sons in the professions
– important members of the 'shopocracy' that ruled Merthyr

under the aegis of the ironmasters. They were also probably the closest approach in nineteenth-century Wales to an English-style middle class.

We do not know where the Lewises settled, or even how many of them arrived in Merthyr. If Lewis Davies, whose account was the earliest on record, is correct and Dic's mother did not long survive his birth,[4] then possibly Elizabeth Lewis was acting as 'mother' for her younger brothers and sister, and presumably John, Matthew and Sarah would still have been with their family. Dic and his father are said to have worked as ironstone miners, in which case the family could have been comparatively well off; ironstone miners were the cream of the workforce in the town (at this point coal miners were in a minority), and the only ones who could afford to purchase gold watches.

If so, we can at least make an informed guess at the kind of home that the Lewises found in Merthyr. Naturally, such a rapid growth in population and the need to provide housing for it led to a great deal of hastily thrown-up, jerry-built accommodation, but the Lewises arrived fairly early in the process and stood a reasonable chance of finding a decent home. We do not know for certain who Lewis Lewis and his son worked for, but it has been suggested that they were employees of the Crawshay family. The Crawshays had a large ironstone mine at Rhyd-y-car which supplied the ironworks at Ynysfach, and near it built homes for their workers, among whom were friends of Dic's. One terrace of six cottages has survived and has been rebuilt at the National Museum of History at St Fagans.[5] We do know that at least one member of Dic's circle of acquaintances, William Morla, lived in Rhyd-y-car.

The Rhyd-y-car houses were built in about 1801, and though they were probably better than the average, they were small and represent the lowest accepted standards as far as the Crawshays were concerned. They were effectively one room upstairs and one down, with an extension downstairs at the back containing the main bedroom and a pantry. Most such cottages had their own gardens, in which the occupants would grow vegetables and keep pigs and poultry. Inside, the rooms were comparatively bare, compared to the clutter of later Victorian times. The floors were bare stone flags and the furniture the plain chairs and tables, settles and benches of the typical country cottage. Perhaps a bacon joint hung from the rafters under the unplastered ceiling of the living room.

Historians tend to stress the inadequacies of the new towns of the Industrial Revolution, and compared to modern expectations this is certainly fair, but in practice these houses were a considerable improvement on the dark, damp, mud-walled cottages of the west Wales countryside from which so many of Merthyr's immigrants had come. Indeed, despite the lack of privies and the general pollution of all kinds from the works, Merthyr at this point was probably a comparatively healthy place in which to live ('comparatively' being very much the operative word). Later on conditions worsened, and the population itself altered as more and more immigrants came into the town from much further afield, but in Dic's time the ordinary people of Merthyr formed a very cohesive, Welsh-based society in which the old sanctions held. 'China', the wild slum enclave where even the authorities feared to go, was still mainly in embryo.

A few years later, in the 1840s, there were a number of reports by government commissioners on the state of education, working conditions and so forth. To some extent, these played up the worst elements of what they found – both human and industrial – because the impulse behind them was to improve the lives of those in the communities they studied (the infamous 'Treason of the Blue Books', the 1847 report on education in Wales whose authors also decided to comment disparagingly on the morals of the Welsh, shows how far the preconceptions of the commissioners could twist the evidence). However, there was an article in the *Westminster Review*[6] in 1848 which perhaps gives a less downbeat view of the people of Merthyr, if not of the town itself.

> The interior of the houses is, on the whole, clean. Food, clothing, furniture – those wants the supply of which depends on the exertions of each individual, are tolerably well supplied. It is those comforts which only a governing body can bestow that are totally absent. The footways are seldom flagged, the streets are ill-paved, and with bad materials, and are not lighted. The drainage is very imperfect, there are few underground sewers, no house drains, and the open gutters are not regularly cleaned out … the refuse is thrown into the streets … The houses are badly built and planned without any regard to the comfort of the tenants, whole families being frequently lodged – sometimes sixteen in number – in one chamber … The colliers are much disposed to be clean, and are careful to wash themselves in the river, but there are no baths, or washhouses, or even waterpipes … in some of the suburbs the people draw their [water] supply from the waste water of the works, and in Merthyr the water is brought by hand from the springs on the hillsides, or lifted from the river, sometimes nearly dry, sometimes a raging torrent, and always charged with the filth of the upper houses and works.

At this point men, women and children still worked together in the ironworks and the mines, in Merthyr as elsewhere. Their lives were dominated by the ironmasters who employed them, who often built their homes, and in Dowlais as time went on, produced a kind of company town with a school, a church, Sunday Schools, a mechanics institute and a truck system (payment of workers with vouchers instead of money), all instituted or built by the Guest family. The Crawshays, though equally dominant, were rather less paternalistic. They did not encourage the truck system (where workers were forced to buy from the company shop, often at inflated prices), but in practice the romantic turrets of Cyfarthfa Castle (built in 1825) presided over the town every bit as firmly as the Guest presence in Dowlais. On the other hand, very little about Merthyr fitted the colourful stereotypes of the historical novelist – the town was unique, in its size, its attitudes and its variety.

In 1819 Dic was 11 or 12 at most, and he is said to have started work in Merthyr with his father as an ironstone miner. This was probably his first full-time job; although quite young children were often employed in the mines and other works as doorkeepers or on the numerous fetching and carrying tasks, the little we hear of Dic's childhood suggests that he was not one of these. As mentioned earlier, since Aberafan was a largely rural community, he may well have worked for one of the local farmers – there is a tradition among the descendants of the Aberafan Portreeve David Jones that the Lewis family as a whole worked on his land before they moved to Merthyr.[7]

Dic must have known that now he was a worker, there was little chance of any more formal education, but he continued to read, perhaps to write, and to listen to his elders as they talked – to absorb anything and everything that came his way. To the uninitiated, working as a miner might not appear to be the most intellectual of careers, but in practice the pattern of the miner's working day allowed a variety of opportunities for debate and discussion of everything from workers' rights to theology. Whether it was this, the long-term effect of all those sermons and Sunday School sessions at Carmel, or his own natural inclination that led him, we do not know, but by the time he was 15, Dic had become so concerned with the oppressions that he and others suffered at the hands of their employers and social superiors that he spoke out against them on behalf of his fellows.[8] One might not have expected the complaints of a 15-year-old boy to be taken seriously or to make any impact, but it seems that they were, and Dic found himself on the wrong side of those in authority. Whether he eventually lost his job as a result or whether he thought it prudent to go away for a time is not clear, but he then spent some time working as a haulier, hauling timber at Llanelley near Brecon.[9] This would have been in about 1825.

It was while Dic was working here that he is said in several accounts to have met the other Lewis Lewis – Lewsyn yr Heliwr, his co-defendant in the 1831 trial – and become friendly with him. Much later, when both men were in prison, one waiting to be transported and the other to be hanged, Lewsyn solemnly swore that he had had no knowledge of Dic before they both found themselves in Cardiff Gaol after the riots. Whether, or how far, this was true is another matter. Although it is not entirely clear whether Lewsyn's nickname of '*yr Heliwr*' referred to him as a huntsman (*heliwr*) or a haulier (*haliwr*), he seems to have had both occupations, and if both men were working in the same area at the same work at the same time, it would seem likely that they did come across each other. On the other hand, Lewsyn was a married man, almost twice Dic's age, and not the most obvious choice as a close friend. In the end the real mystery is why Lewsyn should have wanted, or needed, to make his solemn declaration of ignorance when he himself had already been reprieved and it could serve no purpose for either of them.

By now Dic's household in Merthyr was beginning to change. Both parents, Lewis and Mary Lewis, had dropped out of sight, and John may already have settled at Pyle, working as a lime-burner. Dic was about 19 years old, and if Elizabeth had indeed been acting as mother for the Lewis clan, then perhaps she now felt free to follow her own wishes. At any rate, by 1827 we find that Elizabeth had moved to Newport in Monmouthshire, and Matthew and Sarah perhaps went with her – Sarah certainly was associated with that area in later life. Why exactly Elizabeth went to Newport – whether she went for work or whether she had already met her future husband, perhaps through her chapel connections – is not known, but once in Newport she seems to have become a member of the congregation at Hope Chapel, and in September 1827 she married Morgan Howells, another associate of that chapel.[10] Howells came originally from St Nicholas in the Vale of Glamorgan. He had begun work as a carpenter, but had come under the patronage of Colonel Rowley Lascelles, one of the Morgan dynasty of Tredegar, who helped him to get an education. When he was 16, he went to Newport, where he was converted by the Revd John Rees, minister of Hope Chapel, and took up the Calvinistic Methodist ministry as a career. Hope was an Independent/Congregational chapel and in 1829 Howells founded Ebenezer, also in Newport, as a Calvinistic Methodist, Welsh-language cause. He was to become one of his denomination's great preachers. His biography, published just after his death, is entitled *Boanerges* – the 'Sons of Thunder' of the New Testament: Apostles James and John. In this biography Elizabeth is described as 'loving, gentle and quiet'; her connection with Dic is not overtly mentioned. She and Morgan had six children, but Elizabeth died young, at 41, after 'suffering a terrible illness and bitter trials [possibly a reference to her brother's execution?] in faith and patience.'

Although later writers have tended to assume that Howells, as a Calvinistic Methodist clergyman, was not in sympathy with Dic, they had much in common. Morgan Howells came from a working-class background, he was concerned for the poor, had radical views and supported animal rights. This latter point is interesting because it was said that Dic lost his job as a haulier at Llanelley because of an incident to do with one of the horses. There are no details of what happened, but from what we know of him, it seems most likely that Dic was objecting to ill-treatment of the animal.

Howells was in Newport at the time of the Chartist attack on the town in 1839. His grandson James Evans (Dic's great-nephew) later reported that Howells had gone into town on the morning of the rising and commented when he got home that 'the Chartists have had enough breakfast this morning'.[11] This has always been taken as a criticism of the insurgents, but in the end it depends on the tone in which it was said. In *Requiem For A Patriot* Alexander Cordell notes, quoting a letter from John Foster Geach to the Chartist John Frost, that there had been an attempt to implicate the preacher of Hope Chapel in the rising; 'it failed, and it will raise your spirits to know that ever he prays publicly for your liberation and the downfall of your enemies.'[12] Cordell gives no source for this and 'the preacher of Hope chapel' at that point was the Revd Benjamin Byron, a keen supporter of the anti-slavery movement, but this gives some idea of the ethos of the connection. Morgan Howells was certainly an advocate for his brother-in-law in the earlier unrest, and it is possible that it was partly realisation of their mistake in Merthyr that persuaded the authorities to reprieve Frost and his fellow rebels from their even more grisly fate. Frost's connection with Hope Chapel was clearly important: as a matter of family heritage, some of his descendants have included the name of the chapel as part of their own name even till the present day, e.g. Gerald Hope Frost.

By the spring of 1828 Dic was back in Merthyr. Whether the authorities had forgotten his original radical activities or whether the fact that he was now the brother-in-law of the very respectable, well-known Morgan Howells helped to clear his way back to employment is unknown, but there he was, and about to become a solid family man. He married Elizabeth Harries on 7 April 1828, and the couple settled in the Ironbridge/Ynysgau area of the town. This may be where Elizabeth's family were to be found – there was a Harry family attached to Ynysgau Presbyterian Chapel, and surnames were still fluid at the time. Their son, named Richard after his father, was born at the end of November and baptised at Ynysgau Presbyterian Chapel on 7 January 1829, but sadly died only nine months later and was buried on 13 October of that year.[13] We know very little about Elizabeth Harries, and most of what we do know comes from her second marriage to

Dic's friend John Evans. She died in 1852, aged 49, so she was apparently a few years older than Dic.

The marriage was evidently not welcomed by Dic's family, or at least not by Morgan and Elizabeth; there are various references to their annoyance at the match, though the reasons given vary. One source even suggests that Dic had married Morgan's sister Mari[14] – Howells did have a sister, but her name was Sarah, and she had gone to live in Bristol. In fact there was probably another reason for their disappointment: either Richard junior was a seven-months child or his parents had got married in a hurry. Dic was still very young – about 20 years old – his bride was older than he was, and bearing in mind the general opinion that he was intelligent and knowledgeable, the Howellses may even have hoped that he would follow Morgan into the ministry. Though he was not a regular chapelgoer, everyone agreed that Dic was 'a very moral young man'.[15] Whatever the truth of the matter, the quarrel did not last, because it was his sister and brother-in-law to whom he turned at the end.

Dic and his wife did have a second child, Mary, who was baptised in Cardiff Gaol on 26 July 1831. She outlived her father, but died less than two years later, being buried on 16 March 1833. Three years after that, on 4 March 1836, Dic's widow married Dic's friend, John Evans. She had two more children: Henry, who died young, and another Elizabeth, who was born deaf and dumb but survived, grew up and married, leaving descendants behind her in the Rhondda. This younger Elizabeth was 12 when her mother died, of 'brain paralysis'.[16]

When Dic and his family first came to Merthyr, the town was relatively calm, despite its radical tradition. It had not always been so peaceful.[17] In 1800 there had been serious unrest, due at that point to a combination of rising prices following a poor harvest and the effects of the 'long pay' (payment of wages monthly rather than weekly) and truck systems. Under that latter system, as mentioned earlier, the employer/company would set up a shop which the men were obliged to use – they might even be paid in tokens which could only be used at the company shop, where the prices were often higher than elsewhere. If there was a long gap between paydays, they would not be given cash advances on their pay, but tickets to be used at the shop, the amount to be set against their wages when paid. This could lead to accusations of fraud from the workmen if they felt more had been taken as an advance than they had actually spent in the company shop.

On Saturday, 20 September 1800, workmen from the four ironworks, Penydarren, Dowlais, Cyfarthfa and Plymouth, met and decided to take action to try to lower the price of food. By the following Monday, a mob had gathered and begun to take over the town. They sacked the Penydarren company shop and began to go around the area demanding money, food and drink from the 'respectable', better-off residents. They also obliged shopkeepers to sign agreements promising to sell basic supplies – flour, butter and cheese – at fixed lower prices. The action had drawn in men from Sirhowy and Beaufort, and had spread down the valley to Caerphilly. Meanwhile Homfray had sent for the military from Bristol and Swansea. The Bristol troops were blocked by floods on the River Severn, but 20 Dragoons from Gloucester did arrive, plus a detachment of the Cardiff Yeomanry, and they managed to restore order and arrest some of the ringleaders.

The events at Merthyr reached a wide audience, and on 12 October 1800 the *Shrewsbury Chronicle* reported:

> We find considerable pleasure in informing our readers that the Cardiff Volunteer Cavalry have received the thanks of his Royal Highness the Duke of York, for their promptitude and exertion in quelling the riots at Merthyr Tydfil; and it will be but justice to add, that during the whole of a very severe night, they kept a constant guard, and patrolled the streets and vicinity of that populous town; which greatly tended to restore peace and prevent a rescue of the prisoners then in custody.

There are 23 delinquents now in Cardiff gaol, 20 out on bail, and nearly 100 absconded.

At the Assizes in April 1801 many of those arrested were found not guilty, or given just short periods of imprisonment, but the judge chose to make an example of three of the ironworkers: Aaron Williams, Samuel Hill and James Luke. They were found guilty of assault and theft and sentenced to death. Luke, who was 18 years old, had his sentence commuted to transportation for life but the other two were hanged. In his address to the condemned men, Judge Hardinge admitted that their previous record had been clear of evildoing, but he was particularly harsh in his account of their crimes. He added that his heart bled for them, but that their deaths might save other lives, and if they were properly penitent then they might find forgiveness in the world to come – as long as they forgave those who persecuted them. There is an unpleasant tone of self-righteousness in the speech – but Hardinge was also the judge notorious for his condemnation of Mary Morgan for infanticide at Presteigne, her death sentence an unusually harsh punishment for an unmarried teenager at that time.

The final act of the 1800 riots was also noted by the *Shrewsbury Chronicle* on 29 May 1801, and the report is worth repeating because of its foreshadowing of the events of 1831:

On Friday se'ennight were executed on Cardiff Heath, pursuant to their sentence, Samuel Hill and Aaron Williams, two of the Merthyr rioters, who had been capitally convicted at the late Great Sessions of the County of Glamorgan – They both behaved with the greatest penitence, and seemed fully confident, through the merits of their Redeemer, of having had pardon and forgiveness – Aaron Williams, during the course of his prayers, before they were turned off, observed "that they were going to suffer for hundreds"; Samuel Hill replied "yes, for thousands, but I never knew so happy a day as this in the course of my life."

The two men were clearly aware that they were scapegoats. Perhaps Samuel Hill believed that their fate would somehow spark a new deal for the workers, but if so, he was misled.

After the riots of 1800 there was a period of calm in Merthyr until 1816. That year again saw a season of poor harvests and a rise in prices, and though generally speaking the workmen were well paid, the lay-offs and wage reductions caused by the ups and downs of the iron industry, plus many of the ironworks' use of 'long pay' and the truck system of payment in vouchers tied to expensive company shops, led to unrest in the early summer. Some workers' meetings were held and there were attempts by envoys from Merthyr to gather sympathisers in the works to the east, but soldiers were again sent for and the unrest faded.

Then on Tuesday, 15 October 1816, the workmen at Tredegar were warned of a further wage cut due in November. A delegation from Merthyr arrived that evening, got some of the forgemen to stop work and then, on the Wednesday, went back to Merthyr to stop the four works there. However, not all the crowd stayed together, Josiah John Guest and his fellow ironmasters were able to resist, and by midnight the town was quiet. The Thursday began peacefully, but evidently the crowd from the day before had only gone home for the night. It gathered again and set off east to put out furnaces in that direction, returning to Merthyr by 5 p.m. in an angry mood. In the meantime the ironmasters had enrolled 200 special constables and prepared defences – but the constables fled when they saw the rough mood of the crowd. The ironmasters were stoned, Crawshay hid in a farmhouse and Guest barricaded himself in Dowlais House and shot at the mob, causing several casualties.

On the Friday a crowd of some 5,000 men assembled – not all of them willingly. The authorities gathered at the Castle Inn, sent for the militia and read the Riot Act, but any confrontation was, for the moment, delayed as the crowd set off east again to call out the workers in Tredegar, Blaenavon and beyond, though there was apparently less discontent there. By Saturday 19th the ironmasters had been reinforced. To the original 25 militia men who had arrived earlier were added 30 cavalrymen from Cardiff, other troops had been sent for from Swansea and Newport, and the works were restarted.

The crowd, now consisting of some 8–10,000 workmen, arrived back at the Castle Inn in Merthyr in the early afternoon, at the same time as another 120 soldiers. In a foreshadowing of the events of 1831, a deputation went into the inn to speak with the ironmasters, but were told that they must go home quietly, and only then would the masters treat with them. While this was going on, the lawyer William Meyrick offered refreshments to the crowd. What he offered and whether this was in any way adequate for such a large crowd is another matter, but it gave an opportunity for the soldiers to take up strong defensive positions. The deputation came out and the crowd surged forward in heavy rain to hear the results. At once the Riot Act was read and the crowd were warned to disperse or they would be fired on. When they stayed firm, the cavalry were ordered to charge, using bayonets and the flat of their swords, and the workmen, who only had clubs and sticks to defend themselves, scattered. That was the end of the matter; some thirty members of the crowd were taken prisoner and eight of them were sent off to Cardiff. Two of these were women – although we speak of workmen, it should be remembered that in this period women still worked in mines, tinplate works and ironworks.

There are a number of elements in the 1816 riots which foreshadow the events of 1831, but on the whole it was a less damaging event. Any violence was directed at the works and the ironmasters, and there was not the communal upheaval of the later unrest – hence the use here of 'crowd', rather than 'mob', for those involved. There was a certain degree of compulsion, with men forced to go along with the crowd – but most importantly, the army was not instructed to go in and cut down the protestors. One of the men shot by Guest on the Thursday did die later, but the cavalry charge seems only to have inflicted cuts and bruises. The government had not been embarrassed and there was no need for a display of major penalties after the event.

Although this was before the arrival of unions, there was already a degree of organisation about outbreaks like these. Skilled workmen would meet, often in local inns – perhaps the only place where they could meet without arousing suspicion (hence, possibly, the comment that Dic 'liked his glass'). There they could discuss particular complaints, responses to these and moves against the perceived injustices that faced them. If there was a need for larger-scale action, they could call a mass meeting, bring in the unskilled workmen and make use of their wider network of contacts. One can see this working in 1816, when problems in Tredegar quickly brought a deputation from Merthyr. Meanwhile, the authorities had their own informers and spies. The leaders of the workmen knew these existed, but not who they were, hence the need for solemn oaths binding workers to secrecy (which, of course, was the crime of the Tolpuddle Martyrs).

This is the background against which one can set the intelligent, knowledgeable, charismatic Dic Penderyn. If the marriage certificate on which he only made his mark is for one reason or another misleading and he could write as well as read, then he must have seemed a serious menace, not so much to the ironmasters as to the higher authorities. The French Revolution 30 years earlier might have mutated into Napoleon's dictatorship, but its ideas were not dead in France or in Britain, and every so often they would surface – as they did with the Cato Street Conspiracy of 1820, when Arthur Thistlewood and his associates planned to assassinate the Cabinet. The conspirators were betrayed by a government spy named Edwards, and the authorities seem to have let the plot continue for a while to ensure that they uncovered all the plotters and their plans. Three Scottish radicals were executed at the same time as the Cato Street group, and these were by no means the only serious examples of unrest in the period up to 1831. In these circumstances, the government was obviously going to take an interest in any indication of radical opinions or activities.

There were various ways of dealing with unwanted elements. For instance, they could be sacked, then the Poor Law used to send them back to their original parish of settlement, which could be on the other side of the country. Alternatively, a more permanent way of dealing with the problem was to sentence the most prominent rioters to death, perhaps then commuting their sentences to transportation: a neat combination of punishment and mercy, which also removed them from the scene for the foreseeable future.

We know nothing about Dic's activities at this point. However, it may be significant that in their novels based on events at Merthyr in 1831, both Michael Gareth Llewelyn and Gwyn Thomas show the figure based on Dic as addressing meetings and organising events. They were writing before the creation of Llafur: The Welsh People's History Society and the academic work of Gwyn A Williams, David Jones and others, but both had access to the local traditions of Glamorgan and used them in their work. If they were reflecting these in this case, that could explain why Dic's story had such a wide and long-lasting impact. And such activities were not something to be publicised and put on record: the authorities were paranoid about what they saw as the threat of unions. Rioters were one thing, but a proto-union organiser was a major threat as far as they were concerned.

CHAPTER 3

Riots and Risings

BETWEEN 1817 AND 1830 Merthyr had stayed relatively calm. There had been disturbances in Monmouthshire, and the beginnings of trade unionism as such arrived in the region in early 1830, but did not really reach Merthyr itself until after the riots. On the other hand, 1830 saw the appearance of a much more radical tone in the town, with movements both national – like that for the reform of Parliament – and perhaps of more local interest, like anti-truck and anti-Corn Laws reform. William Crawshay was among the leaders of the movement for Parliamentary reform, pushing for the creation of a Member of Parliament for Merthyr, while 'political union clubs' were set up to discuss these matters. The clubs had a wide range of members, including working men as well as the more obvious middle-class representatives, and political literature – both monthly publications like *Cobbett's Two-penny Trash*, and pamphlets (the latter rather more inflammatory than Cobbett's work) – was circulated. There were also apparently 'agitators' present, who encouraged the workers, so that overall the general picture included a strong popular element as well as the more conservative 'shopocracy' and professional men.

The defeat of the Reform Bill at the end of April 1831 was not welcome news in Merthyr, and it was agreed at a mass meeting of workmen that an 'Illumination' should be held on 1 May, when everyone would be expected to put a candle in their window to show their support for reform. Those who did not were liable to have their windows broken. As it happens, this event gives us our first sight of Dic, though the evidence is retrospective.[1] It seems that there were two groups who clashed in Merthyr Street, near the Bush Inn, and there was a scuffle. Dic was in one group; James Abbott, who later gave evidence against him, was in the other and the two men possibly came to blows. Abbott was heard to declare that he would 'be up with' (get even with) Dic as a result of this. Although this incident was apparently to have such damaging consequences at the trial, neither man seems to have remembered it until they were prompted in July.

At this point there was an election due. One candidate was Colonel Thomas Wood, already the Tory MP for Brecknockshire, who had opposed the recently defeated Reform Bill. William Crawshay led those who supported the reform candidate – Whig John Lloyd Vaughan Watkins – in the election, and on the 8th and 10th of May his workmen and others went round the town demonstrating their objections to Colonel Wood and his supporters. On the 9th a large mob led by Thomas Llewellyn, who was a miner working for Cyfarthfa, attacked the houses of James Stephens, a shopkeeper, and William Thomas, the local squire – stones were thrown and windows broken. The mob also expressed their disapproval of the lawyer William Meyrick. Meyrick had been involved in the earlier disturbances in 1816, when he offered refreshments to the mob, which had perhaps been seen by the men as a delaying tactic while the soldiers who had been called in took up strong positions.

The next day Llewellyn and another man were arrested. J Bruce, the stipendiary magistrate, committed both men to prison in the absence of bail, but a crowd of some three thousand people surrounded the Bush Inn, where the proceedings were being held, and forced Bruce and James Stephens, who was with him and had made the complaint, to release the two

43

men, signing a paper to that effect. This is the first of several mentions of Llewellyn as a leader.[2] A few years later a Thomas Llewellyn was involved in organising one of the three columns that marched on Newport during the Chartist Rising, though whether this was the same man is unknown.

However, this makes us realise how little we know about the workers and their leaders. Llewellyn's only recorded comment, made when Stephens's house was attacked – "Every one who was an enemy to Reform should be hung on the gallows, and [I] would be the man to do it free of expense" – hardly suggests the kind of man who would be favourably looked on by authority. However, he went back to work just as the others had done.

Although political concerns had been important at the beginning of the unrest and continued to be relevant, other themes now also came to the fore. One was a matter of economics: a decline in trade had begun in 1829 and by 1830 furnaces were beginning to shut down. This led to a reduction in wages and an increase in debt among the workers. At first Crawshay kept his workers' wages up, but in March 1831 these were cut and, on 24 May, 84 puddlers were dismissed. The effects of the depression led to the Court of Requests, originally set up as a court for the settlement of small claims without the time-consuming and expensive need to go elsewhere, being seen as a major evil. There were two reasons for this: the increase in debt in the area and the behaviour of the bailiffs who carried out the court's judgements. They would seize property worth far more than the value of the debt concerned, and sell this off, pocketing the difference. The way in which they carried out their duties was also seen as reprehensible. Isaac Evans describes how the bailiffs would harass the women in isolated farmhouses, grabbing the items they were seizing out of the women's hands.[3] And there is the sad tale of the old woman whose bed was seized from under her, leaving her dying on a pile of straw on the floor.

The workmen had already begun to respond to this, and at a meeting on 15 May had decided to invite the men of Monmouthshire to another mass meeting at Twyn y Waun, just to the north-east of Merthyr town, to be held on 30 May. There were some 2,000 people there – mostly ironstone miners, many of whom were Crawshay workmen. At first the meeting went quietly, discussing the reform of Parliament. This was welcomed not simply as a political advance, but also as a means by which ordinary people would find their lives easier, and this connection between reform and hoped-for economic improvements led to 'Bread and cheese' being one of the main slogans of the Rising from the beginning. There was a motion to draw up a petition thanking the King for the reforms he had brought them, but this failed and the tone of the meeting changed. Now speakers began to discuss the evils of the Court of Requests, and there were complaints about working practices and the behaviour of the parish officers responsible for providing poor relief. Finally the workers voted to withdraw their labour and the meeting dispersed. Whether Dic was present at the meeting we do not know, but it would seem a strong possibility.

The degrees by which the Twyn y Waun meeting morphed into mob rule across Merthyr are undefined, but it may be significant that the site of the meeting was next to the Waun Fair, then taking place. While some of the matters being discussed petered out after the initial reform debate, others (such as working practices) were of more immediate relevance to the men's working lives, while others, like the misdeeds of the Court of Requests and failings in parish relief, were more domestic. Curiously, 31 May appears to have been quiet. Perhaps the workmen were discussing their next moves, while for others the more immediate irritants of debt and bullying officials were being aired and beginning to lead to action.[4]

1 June saw a number of developments. Firstly, a number of the workmen, led by Thomas Llewellyn, headed to Aberdare

to confront the Fothergills, local ironmasters, and try to get them to withdraw comments they had made to the effect that the wages that Crawshay was paying to his miners were too high. Meanwhile, the houses of several of the bailiffs who worked for the Court of Requests were attacked. Finally, Lewis Lewis, Lewsyn yr Heliwr, was drawn into the riots.[5] In June 1831 he was living on Blaencadlan Farm in Penderyn. When bailiffs from the Court of Requests arrived to seize some of his property in lieu of money he owed, a group of Lewsyn's neighbours objected. Next they took back a chest belonging to Lewsyn which had been seized and was by then in a shop in Penderyn, and this then became a kind of portable platform which he carried with him and from which he addressed his followers. Lewsyn was clearly a charismatic figure and someone who saw himself as a leader, though whether he had previously been involved in any movement for workers' rights is unknown. Now he led his group on a march around the area to repossess other people's lost possessions, joining up with others in Merthyr itself.

Historian David Jones, in his account of the riots,[6] suggests that it was the working men of the town who made up the mob, but Bruce, the stipendiary magistrate who had been forced to let Thomas Llewellyn go and who witnessed an attack on Thomas Lewis's premises, claimed in *The Cambrian* that the mob was largely made up of 'women, boys and very young workmen'. Thomas Llewellyn was also at this attack, but at this point he was evidently not part of the mob as such – his wife was one of the crowd attacking Thomas Lewis's house when he arrived in his working clothes, on the way home from the mine. Perhaps, like John Phelps, one of those on trial later, he had been called in to support his wife. As we have seen, the day before he had been leading the workmen to Aberdare, in a successful attempt to get the Fothergills to retract their ill-advised comments on wage rates, but the men appear to have returned to work after that.

This surely demonstrates the existence of two elements in what happened at Merthyr. Firstly there were the activities of those like Thomas Llewellyn and the other workmen who were interested in political reform and improved working conditions, and secondly there was a much more traditional element: the demand for communal justice, which a few years later led to the Rebecca Riots. It was not so much the Court of Requests itself that was seen as oppressive, as the behaviour of its officers. It is also worth noting that these initial 'riots', as distinct from the workers' defence of Merthyr that followed, were an area where the women were particularly conspicuous. Often their husbands were there too – and it was chiefly they who later stood trial – but the wives were actively involved in taking back items that had been seized by the bailiffs. It is worth looking at the kind of objects that were being reclaimed too. Mostly the court proceedings only say 'goods', but in one or two cases they are more specific: pictures, watches, a clock, a chest of drawers, a bedstead, soap, two silver spoons, a tea caddy, a Bible. In Thomas Lewis's case, the rioters demanded two guineas, to be refunded to the person who had since bought one of the repossessed items, but generally what was wanted were household items – objects, perhaps, of importance or sentimental value to their original owners. Life was not easy, but those who had been drawn into Merthyr for work were sometimes able, when trade was good and wages a little above the minimum, to afford minor luxuries like framed pictures or family Bibles, and losing these was particularly painful.

The case of John Phelps is interesting here. He was a shoemaker, and he was at work when the mob arrived and told him and his wife to go and reclaim his goods from one Thomas Williams, the sheriff's bailiff. He apparently went on working, but his wife set off and he was 'persuaded to go after her, lest some mischief be done'.[7] At Thomas Williams's house the mob broke down the door and Phelps and his wife went in. Williams's wife Jane met them in the front room and asked what they wanted, to which Phelps replied that he wanted 'a watch, a Bible and his goods' – items which the Williamses had bought some two years before, at an auction.[8] If she did not hand them over, he said, the mob would come in and tear her to pieces. Mrs Phelps went to the parlour, collecting two pictures from the wall, a pound of soap, a tea caddy, two silver spoons and the Bible. Meanwhile the mob came into the house and Jane Williams fainted.

When this case went to trial, the jury returned a verdict of not guilty of breaking into the house, but guilty of theft and of terrifying Jane Williams, and Phelps was sentenced to be transported for 14 years. Two things are clear from this case: firstly, how far the riots were a matter of compulsion by the mob – though 'mob', the word the authorities used, is perhaps not quite correct. That suggests a totally out-of-control crowd of lawbreakers, but though their behaviour could be violent and frightening, and some members of the crowd undoubtedly did get carried away, there was an underlying sense that they were carrying out communal justice in restoring property to the original owners. Secondly, as has been suggested earlier, the 'riots', as distinct from the workers' defence of Merthyr that followed, were in many ways a matter for the women. This was something that the judge confirmed in his sentencing of Joan Jenkins and her two sons. He commented that 'it is too well known that upon these late occasions women took very active parts in these proceedings ... however we may all be disposed to feel for their sex, they are answerable for the crimes they commit.' Joan Jenkins was given twelve months' hard labour; her sons, who had supposedly been influenced by her, got six months' hard labour – which for all three was rather better than the death sentence that the judge chose not to pass. Another of the women who ended up on trial was Margaret Davies, who was also awarded twelve months' hard labour. Historians, concentrating on workers' rights and the growth of unions, have mostly written the women out of the story, but working-class wives and mothers were never the delicate flowers of middle-class legend.

It was, of course, likely that those on trial would want to suggest that they had been forced to join the mob, but there is independent testimony to that compulsion. Isaac Evans's father had been walking along with his friend William Morla near Hirwaun when they ran into the mob and were forced to go along with them, caught up in their ropes.[9] Isaac's father slipped away, but the crowd saw him go and chased him into a disused incline in the hillside. They blocked him in with rocks, and moved on, leaving him trapped. William Morla waited for a better opportunity, then slipped away himself, went back and freed Isaac's father. The community in Merthyr at that point was still not too far from its rural origins, and as has been suggested, the ropes are an intriguing echo of those traditionally used by village children to oblige onlookers to pay up at weddings. Indeed, as was also suggested earlier, it seems that the Merthyr 'riots' were in many ways an expression of natural justice, a means of punishing those who had offended against the moral code of the community. One thinks of the *ceffyl pren*, the 'skimmity ride' of Thomas Hardy's *The Mayor of Casterbridge*, used to shame a sinner. Undoubtedly in Merthyr there were those who took advantage and plundered their victims, rather than trying to set right what they saw as injustice, and for others their sense of moral justification allowed a degree of violence in words or behaviour that they would not otherwise have accepted. But those were the downsides of what were otherwise the means by which decent order was kept in a world without police forces.

On the whole there was little or no actual looting involved. The attack on Thomas Lewis's house seems to have been at least partly inspired by an attempt to insist on fair dealing. A widow who had bought a confiscated chest of drawers for two guineas had seen it repossessed by the crowd; now Lewsyn insisted that Thomas Lewis repay the money so she could be reimbursed. Although Lewsyn was one of the leaders of the riots, urging the mob on in the confrontation on the following day, he also to some extent acted as a restraining influence – something that was to save his life later on. He was not the only person to profit in this way. John Morgan was involved in an attack on Philip Taylor, one of the shopkeepers, but he had also stopped anyone from harming Taylor, who spoke up for him at his trial. Morgan thus avoided a possible death sentence, being given twelve months' hard labour instead.

The houses of the bailiffs of the Court of Requests were attacked on 1 June, but it was not until the next day that the house of Joseph Coffin, Clerk of the Court, was attacked (among those indicted for this was the previously mentioned Margaret Davies) and the records of the Court of Requests burned. By this time the authorities had begun to gather at the Castle Inn, situated in the centre of Merthyr. A number of houses had been attacked and now the tradesmen came to ask that soldiers be sent for to restore order. By the evening it was clear that this must be done, and troops were summoned from Brecon.

At this point there was no professional police force available. There were parish constables, who dealt with local law and order matters such as escorting paupers back to their own parish, or seeing that innkeepers obeyed the trading standards regulations, but these were hardly adequate when there was major unrest. At times like these, magistrates could enrol numbers of special constables – as they had done in the past in Merthyr – but these men were ordinary citizens, usually of the respectable classes, with no training in law enforcement. If major unrest threatened, then soldiers were called in to police the community concerned. However, the presence of armed troops could lead to unfortunate results, as it had done at Peterloo a few years before. James Abbott was a special constable, while John Thomas (Shoni Crydd) was a parish constable. Both were to play a part later on.

Overnight the mob turned to enrolling the workmen, going first to Cyfarthfa, and then to Penydarren, Dowlais and Plymouth to get the men out. By 7 a.m. there was a large crowd parading round Merthyr town, using ropes to corral those they drew in and stop them from escaping. By 10 a.m. they were moving towards Cyfarthfa again, but on the way they met William Crawshay and the detachment of the 93rd Highlanders who had been summoned from Brecon. The mob duly 'escorted' the soldiers into town – to the Castle Inn, which was once again, as in 1816, the base for the magistrates and other authorities. There, after putting down their packs, the main body of the soldiers was stationed outside the inn but with a gap between them and the wall, while a smaller group were inside the Castle, on the first floor.

As it happens, there is a drawing of the Castle Inn and the area round it, made some ten or fifteen years later, which enables us to picture the scene on that morning of 3 June (see photo section). The Castle Inn was on a corner, overlooking what appears to be a widening in the road sufficient to allow for a considerable crowd to gather. The inn itself evidently began as a typical country town hostelry and looks like a child's drawing of a house, with the front door in the centre, a window on each side, and three windows in a row on the first floor. By the look of it, with the growth of the town and the need for accommodation for visitors, this had been extended on the left-hand side of the building, providing a three-storey addition. Next to this was the Castle Vaults, what we would now call an off-licence, selling wines and spirits; a woman and child are coming out of this in the image. Next to that was James Abbott's barber shop, with a white-aproned figure in the door. The main entrance to the inn is simple: an ordinary shop doorway, up three steps from the pavement. A man standing on the top step takes up most of the space, though a smaller figure may be coming out of the inn behind him. Either way, there is very little room for scuffling rioters.

At 10.40 a.m. the Riot Act (a 1714 Act of Parliament which authorised local authorities to declare any group of twelve or more people to be unlawfully assembled, and the reading of which meant they must disperse or face punitive action) was read. This formally gave the mob assembled outside the inn, which seems to have numbered several thousand by now, an hour in which to disperse.

Just after this, ironmaster Anthony Hill proposed that a deputation should be sent in from the crowd gathered outside to meet with the ironmasters. Twelve men – Dic amongst them – were selected from among the mob, which by now included the men who had come from the ironworks. Hill later noted that these men had asked for the abolition of the Court of Requests and reductions in the price of bread and in the cost of various other articles, plus an increase in wages, but the meeting then foundered on the ironmasters' determination not to deal with the requests until the mob had dispersed. The members of the deputation, however, knew that the mob would insist on immediate concessions, and they left after fifteen minutes or so. Dic and at least one of the others went out through the back door of the Castle Inn after the meeting.[10]

There is no record of the names of those who made up the deputation, though we know from later evidence that Dic was among them. How they were selected is also unknown. Gwyn A Williams suggests that the group was merely picked at random from the crowd, so Dic being one of the twelve was a matter of chance and does not signify that he had any importance as a leading figure in the movement for social justice. This seems unlikely. Even if the choice of the deputation was ad hoc, those chosen would surely have been at least recognisable as acceptable spokesmen. And, interestingly, Lewsyn was not included, which suggests that the choice was perhaps more directed, more relevant to the political organisation that lay behind activities like those of Thomas Llewellyn and his fellows.

Not surprisingly, the mob was unhappy when it saw the deputation come out empty-handed. Lewsyn, as noted, had not been among those chosen for the deputation, and now he hung on to a lamp iron (a metal bracket for a gas lamp) and tried to speak, though initially with no success. The mob asked ironmaster Josiah John Guest to tell them what had happened at the meeting and there was a to-and-fro exchange, with Guest speaking from an upstairs window, telling them that he would only listen to complaints once they had dispersed, and various members of the crowd saying that they were in need of sufficient wages to buy bread and other supplies for their families. Crawshay echoed Guest, again insisting that the mob should go home if they wanted their complaints to be heard. Then Bruce, the magistrate, announced that the hour's grace given by the Riot Act was up.

This time Lewsyn was able to make himself heard, and he urged the mob to attack the soldiers. With such a large crowd, there was a great deal of pressure anyway, so the soldiers on the ground outside the Castle Inn could not aim their weapons. Though their bayonets were fixed, even these could not easily be deployed. As for the mob, they were not armed as such, but many of them had sticks and clubs – enough to do some damage if it came to a fight. Then, at about noon, there was a rush on the soldiers led by Lewsyn and his associates, who urged the crowd to seize the weapons of the Highlanders. In the fierce fighting that followed, a number of the soldiers were hurt, as were some of the rioters, the inn was almost stormed, and finally the soldiers, now mostly disarmed, withdrew into the inn passage under a hail of stones.

At that point, with the inn seemingly under siege, the order was given for those soldiers who had remained inside the Castle Inn, at the upper windows, to fire on the crowd. A number of people were hit – around a hundred, Gwyn A Williams claims. Some were killed, others so badly wounded that they died later, and the dead included several innocent bystanders – one of them an old woman, sitting knitting in her house across the road. This was enough for the mob, who began to disperse. One group apparently tried to attack from the rear of the inn, but they were repelled by an officer and three soldiers, who fired on them, wounding some and driving off the rest. In 15 minutes or so the mob had vanished, leaving just the dead and wounded to be carried away. The total death toll is unknown – it was said that some of the badly wounded died later and were buried secretly to avoid repercussions – but at least 16 men and women died, and this was clearly the lowest estimate.

Lewsyn and his friends, who had been at the heart of the fighting, seem to have escaped unscathed, but rather than simply going home, as might have been expected, they took the weapons they had seized from the soldiers and began to look for ammunition for them. They retreated to the 'Tip', a cinder bank behind the Castle Inn, and fired down from there. They were too well covered for the Highlanders to drive them off, and so the soldiers formed themselves into groups and patrolled the now empty streets instead.

Why this should have happened is not entirely clear. With so many dead – at least 16, perhaps 24 – one might have expected all the survivors to run for cover, as many evidently did. Things had now gone well beyond the response to an outbreak of communal protest. But perhaps it was precisely the scale of what had happened, the number killed and wounded, that left men like Lewsyn feeling that they had no option but to defend themselves against an authority that had turned on them.

From then on there was a change in the tone of the action. In place of the riotous mob of previous days, there began to be a sense of organisation in what happened next. Lewsyn and others gathered on the canal bridge and started to make arrangements to collect more ammunition for the weapons they had seized and to ensure that the guns were in the hands of those who knew how to use them. There may well have been ex-soldiers among the workers – men like John Phelps, who had been a soldier before he took up the trade of shoemaker.

The Highlanders had come from Brecon, and were likely to be followed by their supply train, containing baggage and ammunition, so now the men headed for Cefn-coed-y-cymmer on the Brecon road, to set up defences there. Meanwhile Bruce and Hill had set off to the south, to Cardiff and beyond, to ask for more soldiers. The Highlanders withdrew to the stronger defensive position of Penydarren House, and in the late afternoon they were joined by a detachment of the Glamorgan Militia from Cardiff and two troops of yeomanry. By 4 June the 'riots' had begun to turn into a 'rising'. In the area of Hirwaun and Aberdare there were groups of workmen forcing the owners of shops there to hand over arms and ammunition, but elsewhere the main concern was to prevent reinforcements from arriving from either Brecon or Swansea. A detachment of cavalry from Swansea was ambushed and their weapons added to the workers' store. In the afternoon there were a series of meetings between the ironmasters and the workers which seem to have been concerned with the men's demands. There was a temporary agreement on these and at least some of the crowd dispersed.

The violence in the area west of Merthyr, round Hirwaun and Aberdare, had also seen one of the iconic moments of the affair, when a flag had been washed in the blood of a calf to create supposedly the first red flag associated with the workers – though in fact red flags and reform banners had been prominent in the earlier attacks on 2 June. However, this area apart, Sunday 5 June was relatively quiet, with various groups travelling to nearby towns to get their workmen out, which meant that by early Monday morning (6 June) a huge assemblage of men had gathered at the Waun. These then proceeded towards Dowlais, where they met the soldiers and John Josiah John Guest, who was able to persuade them to disperse. This might seem strange, but there was always a strong element of compulsion in what went on, and not all of the large numbers of workmen involved were willing participants. The most militant, however, set off to join the men on the Brecon road, where they were carrying out arms drill and preparing to defend Merthyr against the authorities. But in the end there was no battle, and as more soldiers arrived in Merthyr, the crowd slowly melted away, abandoning their weapons. On the Tuesday (7 June) the authorities began the business of rounding up the chief culprits, some of whom had fled as far as Pembrokeshire and Carmarthenshire. Lewsyn was arrested in a wood in Penderyn parish.

It is at this point that we find the first mention of Dic Penderyn, in The Cambrian's list of rioters who had been arrested, interrogated and sent down to Cardiff Gaol in coaches, 'escorted by parties of foot soldiers and the 3rd Dragoon guards.'[11] There were ten men in this first group: six are named, and Dic comes third, after Lewsyn and David Jones, a.k.a. Dai Solomon. He is down as 'Richard Lewis, alias Dic Penderrin'. In the evidence later given in court he is not mentioned among those engaged in the attacks on Thomas Lewis or Thomas Williams, nor in the general mayhem of those few days, only with regard to the wounding of soldier Donald Black, who had been stabbed in the thigh.

It is thanks to the careful gathering of evidence about Dic's movements on the morning of 3 June by Joseph Tregelles Price, a Quaker ironmaster from Neath known for his charitable work, that we know what he did.[12] Dic was one of the deputation of twelve who went into the Castle Inn to meet the ironmasters, and when that ended, he left the inn by the back door along with another of the deputation, a man called Johns. This may have been the John Winford whom Dic himself said in the trial had come out with him – perhaps 'Winford' was actually a nickname like Penderyn, rather than a surname. Dic then stood by the taproom window, talking to Nancy Evans and her son for 15 or 20 minutes, until they heard the first gunshot.

At that, Dic, young Evans, plus another man called Benjamin Davies and possibly others, ran off down Glebe Lane, through the archway (a local landmark) and across the Iron Bridge. A number of witnesses confirmed that they had seen Dic at the back of the Castle Inn. David Abraham, who was one of the special constables, said he had seen Dic in front of the inn, presumably before the deputation went in, and had warned him about 'going forward', but did not believe that Dic was in the front of the crowd later on, at the time of the stabbing.

What happened then is obscure. The Lewis family tradition held that Dic went to ground on Aberdare Mountain during the next three or four days, and this is supported by Isaac Evans,[13] who stated that Dic was hiding out on the mountain, away from the rioters, with Isaac's uncle, John Evans. Earlier that year Dic had had an argument with one of the special constables, John Thomas, better known as Shoni Crydd, which had left the constables 'suspicious' of him, and he was afraid that he would be one of the first to be accused now that they had an excuse to do so. Whether Dic and John Evans (who later married Dic's widow) spent all the time hiding out on their own or whether they at any point became caught up in the activities of the workers is unknown. Dic always denied stabbing Donald Black, but there is a certain ambiguity about his admission of other sins – was he speaking of moral failures or of being part of the workers' campaign? Either way, the two men eventually decided that it was time to go home. John Evans went first, and arrived safely. Dic waited till later, perhaps until it was dark and he was less likely to be picked up by any passing representatives of the law. It was about 10 or 11 o'clock when he reached home and went to bed. The special constables had already called at the house earlier, to find him absent; now, sometime around midnight, they came back and arrested him in his bed, taking him off to the 'Dark House' to join their other prisoners. They were all then taken to Penydarren to be interrogated at the Ivy Bush Inn. Dic was there until Friday, 10 June, when he was one of the first batch of prisoners to be taken down to Cardiff to await trial at the forthcoming Assizes, due that July.

What, if anything, the men involved in the Rising – as distinct from the rioters of the first two or three days – had hoped to achieve is hard to know. There were suggestions at the time that the events in Merthyr had been part of a planned much wider, even national, rising, but there does not appear to be any evidence to support this. For many, it was improved pay and working conditions that they hoped to see, and which they demanded in their various meetings with the ironmasters. They may have felt that it was necessary to go beyond mere negotiations if they were to get results. Probably too, there was a degree of anger at seeing their fellow townspeople shot down by the soldiers which encouraged Lewsyn and his fellows to fight back and turn a riot into a rising. Then there was the example of risings in France and elsewhere in the previous year. As to the disintegration of the Rising, there was always a divide between the serious militants like Lewsyn and his associates and those others who were drawn in by immediate enthusiasm or crowd pressure and were happy to go home when the chance came. Yet however mixed the motives behind the Merthyr Rising, it did mark a significant stage in the growth of a working-class identity, with its own strengths and ambitions.

CHAPTER 4

The Trial

JUSTICE IN THE early nineteenth century was still in many ways in a state of flux, particularly as regards the position of the defendant in a trial. In earlier centuries the active part had been played by the judge, the prosecution and the jury. The defendant would be present, but almost as an onlooker, basically because it was felt that if they were allowed to testify, they might be tempted to lie on oath and so endanger their immortal soul. Instead, the judge would act as a sort of proxy defence, cross-questioning the witnesses and preventing any obvious bias against the defendant.

> Hanoverian judges [and the Merthyr trials were pre-Victorian] worked within a criminal justice system which quite purposefully upheld propertied hierarchy first and delivered justice second … in which judges and home secretaries *had* to placate great men even if not to capitulate to them, in which juries were often timid, mercy grudging, pardons rare, and compensation for wrongful punishment unthinkable.[1]

In practice Lewsyn and Dic seem to have been fortunate. Their judge, Mr Justice Bosanquet, was willing to look again at the circumstances of their case, and the jury, in Lewsyn's case at least, did not simply rubber-stamp a verdict that they must have known was expected.

As to counsel for the defence, few defendants could afford this, and if they could, these were usually chosen 'at random on the day of the trial from among the junior barristers who ... would traipse the circuit behind the judge and leaders. Perhaps over half had no counsel at all. The most casual efforts were made to ensure that the defendants' witnesses attended the trial, however life-threatening the charge.'[2] In the case of the Merthyr rioters, they did have counsel – it would seem that William Crawshay paid for this. Perhaps he felt a degree of, if not guilt, perhaps responsibility for having encouraged debate about reform. On the other hand, though Henry Sockett[3] (who led the defence) was agreed to have done his best for his clients, he is obscure, to say the least, whereas William Henry Maule (who led the prosecution) was in the middle of a highly distinguished career which saw him in the eight years after these trials become an MP and a knight, and he later became a Privy Councillor. It is possible that Crawshay or his representatives had had some difficulty in finding an expert barrister willing to defend the rioters and risk official wrath if they were too successful. Equally, it is likely that with such a serious breach of the peace, the authorities had picked a particularly experienced and skilful candidate to deal with the prosecution.

Even apart from this, there were serious limitations on what the defence knew or could do.[4] There was no disclosure beforehand of evidence or of the names of witnesses for the prosecution, and the defendant might not even know before the start of the trial exactly what they were charged with. Neither could they go into the witness box to give evidence on their own behalf, though they could cross-question the witnesses. In felony cases, the defence counsel could not sum up for the jury at the end of the proceedings, before they considered their verdict. If any statement was made, it would not be recorded. There were soon to be changes, and after 1836 the defendant had at least more access to the charges and the evidence against them, though they could still not go into the witness box themselves until 1898. Anglican cleric and writer Sydney Smith, writing in 1828, gives us some idea of the situation in which Dic and his fellows found themselves:

> How are they to obtain witnesses? ... The witnesses are fifty miles off, perhaps totally uninstructed ... utterly unable to give up their daily occupation, to pay for their journey, or for their support when arrived at the town of trial – and if they could get there, not knowing where to go, or what to do. It is impossible but that a human being, in such a helpless situation, must be found guilty; for as he cannot give evidence for himself, and has not a penny to fetch those who can give it for him, any story told against him must be taken for true (however false).[5]

Although prosecution witnesses could be paid for their attendance, there was no such arrangement for defence witnesses. A similar drawback also applied to the depositions being collected for the prosecution. Although notionally the prisoner could be present when these were taken, it was most unlikely that this would be a practical possibility. The authorities were hardly going to arrange for prisoners in Cardiff to go jaunting off to Merthyr, where William Meyrick was interviewing the witnesses. In the circumstances, it is not surprising that there were no serious defence witnesses in any of the Merthyr trials, and no attempt to prove that any of the accused had not been there or carried out the acts of which they were accused. There were two or three character witnesses, but that was all.

The events that had occurred in Merthyr Tydfil in early June 1831 were of interest not only in the town itself, but throughout south Wales and beyond. There are three contemporary accounts of the trials of the rioters: the official record of the trials taken down by a court recorder; a transcript of the evidence for the prosecution in the case of Dic and Lewsyn taken by the lawyer William Meyrick, dated 14 June and later sent to the Home Secretary, Lord Melbourne; and the account in *The Cambrian* newspaper. Generally speaking, the three accounts agree reasonably well, though each has something of its own to add to the overall picture.[6]

The proceedings against the Merthyr prisoners formed only part of the calendar of that particular session of the Glamorgan Assizes, and *The Cambrian* also included brief summaries of the seven cases dealt with at Neath before the court turned to the Merthyr rioters.[7] Although there was nothing remarkable about these particular cases, they – and the sentences they attracted – do help to provide a context for the Merthyr trials that followed.

Most of the seven cases concerned burglary and/or theft. Thomas Rowland, a mason, stole a hat and a bonnet and was sentenced to seven years' transportation; William Williams, David Davies, Thomas Phillips, Mary Corvice and Lucretia Davies were all found guilty of theft and sentenced to death, but promised that their sentences would be commuted to transportation. (David Davies, a butcher who stole 'a ram and other sheep', was recommended to mercy because of his previous good character and William Williams, also usually of good character, had been drunk at the time when he stole John Greenhouse's boots, but Thomas Phillips and the two women had broken into a house and stolen £14 in silver, with apparently no mitigating circumstances.) As for the other three cases, Francis Jones and another William Williams were found guilty of theft and sentenced to six months hard labour, David Morgan was sentenced to two years' imprisonment for the attempted rape of a 14-year-old girl, and William John received seven years' transportation for sending a threatening anonymous letter to the Hon. W B Grey. The impression that one gets is that at this point the law's bark was considerably worse than its bite – not that transportation was in any sense an easy option, but it could be survived (and it was, of course, very useful in building up a population in the more far-flung reaches of the budding British Empire).

Having dealt with these cases, the Judge, the Hon. Mr Justice Bosanquet, turned to the prisoners from Merthyr. *The Cambrian* reported these proceedings in much greater detail than those mentioned above, often in the witnesses' own words. However, since the reporter gives only the actual evidence – the witnesses' answers, not the questions they were asked – the reports can at first sight be confusing. *The Cambrian* reported four of the trials in some detail, and another four more briefly, as well as mentioning that some prisoners pleaded guilty and were sentenced. In fact it seems that there were some eleven cases recorded in the court records; four of these do not appear in *The Cambrian,* and at least one of the cases mentioned in *The Cambrian* does not appear in the court list.

The first of the trials reported in the newspaper was that of John Phelps, for theft; followed by the trial of David Thomas (Dai Llawhaearn) for riotous assembly and forcibly entering houses and stealing from them. The third trial was announced more formally: 'The King v Lewis Lewis (the Huntsman), David Hughes, Thomas Llewellyn, David Williams, David Thomas, David Jones and Thomas Vaughan were indicted for stealing two sovereigns, watches and other articles from Thomas Lewis's house, of Merthyr.' Interestingly enough, no evidence seems to have been given that Lewsyn was involved in the actual theft, though several witnesses reported seeing him in the street, standing on a chest and urging on the crowd to force Thomas Lewis to refund the two sovereigns to 'a poor widow' (as mentioned in the previous chapter, the actual amount required was two guineas). No one placed Lewsyn in the house.

Possibly the prosecution realised that the evidence so far was unlikely to convict Lewsyn of the actual charges, which were of theft, not incitement. If so, they were unintentionally helped by the defence. Mr Sockett, the chief defence counsel, evidently felt that his best course lay in showing that Thomas Lewis himself was a dubious character who had also been involved in the rioting. He obliged him to admit that he had been in custody for passing bad coin and for selling marbles in place of bullets, and also for supplying gunpowder to the mob. However, Thomas Lewis excused himself from the latter crime by saying that Lewsyn had forced him at gunpoint. This had happened after the attack on the soldiers outside the Castle Inn, and the implication was that Lewsyn's gun was one of the soldiers' muskets. Thomas Lewis added that Lewsyn had also forced him to join the mob who were firing down on the soldiers from the Tip behind the Castle Inn, though Thomas Lewis had run away later. Mr Sockett apparently made no further attempt to discredit Thomas Lewis's evidence. Indeed, the only comment from the defence seems to have come from Lewsyn himself when he asked William Thomas, a local squire who was giving evidence about the behaviour of the crowd when the Riot Act was read outside Thomas Lewis's house, if Thomas remembered him coming to collect a hound. This, too, backfired, since William Thomas said, "No, I remember your coming there and stealing a dog from my kennel."

At the end of this trial the judge ordered that David Williams be acquitted because the mob had forced him to be there. Bosanquet then suggested that the evidence against Thomas Llewellyn and David Jones was not strong – Llewellyn at least may well have been caught up in the mob as he went home, rather than being part of it voluntarily. Furthermore, two character witnesses had testified on behalf of Jones and Llewellyn – one of these being Crawshay's under-manager, Henry Kirkhouse. The jury duly found both men not guilty. As for Lewsyn, Thomas Vaughan, David Hughes and David Thomas (the last of whom had also already been found guilty in the previous trial), all four were found guilty and sentenced to death, but recommended to mercy 'in consequence of its being a riot'.

The curious thing is that, as reported in *The Cambrian*, the trial had very little to do with the charges in the indictment. Thomas Vaughan came into the house and knocked down Thomas Lewis, and David Hughes and David Thomas uttered numerous threats and incitements to violence against the magistrates and others, but as regards the theft of the two sovereigns (or guineas) and the watches, the names mentioned were Robert Jones and Gwenllian Pardoe, neither of whom were on trial. Perhaps the reporter for *The Cambrian* got the indictment wrong. At any rate, Mr Justice Bosanquet's sentencing speech did state, almost in passing, that Vaughan, Hughes and Thomas had been found guilty of robbery with violence, but he then went on to describe at some length their leading role in inciting and directing the mob. What also seems strange to the modern reader is the lack of any serious defence, though possibly it was felt that the offences had been too public to be denied and the only course left to the defence lawyer was to attempt to gain mercy for his clients on grounds of good character (or, with regard to Thomas Lewis, the bad character of the victim).

The fourth trial, as given in *The Cambrian*[8] (the third in the court record), now followed, and Richard Lewis and Lewis Lewis were indicted 'for having stabbed Donald Black, a private in the 93rd regiment (Highlanders) with intent to maim him (the underlining of the last five words in *The Cambrian*'s report was presumably meant to emphasise the fact that the stabbing was deliberate, not just something that occurred in the general chaos of the fighting). The transcript later sent to Lord Melbourne was more specific: 'The Prisoners were indicted that they on 3 June 1831 at the parish of Merthyr Tydfil, with a bayonet affixed to a certain gun which the said Richard Lewis held in both his hands, one Donald Black in and upon the right hip did stab, cut, wound with intent in doing so and malice aforethought to kill and murder the said Donald Black'. A new jury was sworn in for this case.

The trial began with Mr Maule, once again chief counsel for the prosecution, outlining the case against the two Lewises. He described Lewis Lewis as exhorting the crowd to disarm the soldiers, and Richard Lewis, 'a very powerful man', as seizing a musket from Donald Black and stabbing the soldier in the right hip with his own bayonet. The two Lewises then continued to fight 'with desperation' until almost all the rioters had fled, he told the court. Maule added that there had sometimes been as many as three rioters struggling with one soldier for his musket.

The chief prosecution witness, James Abbott, was then called. Abbott was a barber and also a newly enrolled special constable – and the man who had sworn to get even with Dic about a month before the riots. He had seen a small crowd at about 6.30 a.m. on the morning of 3 June, and knew that some or all of this group had gone to Plymouth Works 'to stop the men there from working', but by ten o'clock the crowd in the middle of Merthyr was much larger and parading the streets. The soldiers arrived outside the Castle Inn at about half past ten, to face a very numerous crowd – he estimates about 8–10,000 – 'comprised of working men' (perhaps the workers from the Plymouth Works had joined them). As we know from the later drawing, Abbott's barber's shop was next door to the Castle Inn, though at this point or shortly after Abbott, as a special constable, was apparently in the passage of the inn, and heard the reading of the Riot Act. He saw Lewsyn in the crowd while the discussions were going on indoors between the workers' deputation and the ironmasters. For the moment the crowd was quiet, but once the deputation had come out of the inn, seeming 'very much dissatisfied', Lewsyn began to harangue his followers; he was holding on to a 'lamp iron' and supported on the shoulders of the crowd. Lewsyn was speaking Welsh, which Abbott did not understand. Then 'immediately after Lewis hung by the lamp post, the soldiers were beaten very much'.

It was at this point that Abbott named Richard Lewis for the first time. The barber stated that he 'saw Richard Lewis struggling with the soldier as the latter was making his way into the Inn and whilst he was on the top step, witness saw Richard Lewis wound him with the bayonet fixed on the musket'. Abbott took the soldier by the arm and took him into the brewhouse – the man bleeding profusely. Abbott added that he 'Had not the slightest doubt as to his stab having been given by Richard Lewis'. *The Cambrian*'s account is ambiguous as to who was on the top step, but the prosecution transcript makes it clear that this was Black, not Abbott.

Mr Sockett, as chief defence counsel, then cross-examined James Abbott.

> S: Before the soldiers came, you had not seen Richard Lewis or Lewis Lewis?
> A: Not to the best of my knowledge.

Next, Abbott was questioned about the delegation.

> A: At the time they went in I was outside in the street.
> S: Did you see them go out?
> A: I saw a number come out.
> S: You did not see them go in?
> A: No.

Sockett took Abbott through his evidence again, drawing out a few details as to who spoke when, the general quietness of the mob and their request for bread and cheese. This point was pursued at some length. It seemed that while Lewsyn was speaking, another man – a workman – was addressing Mr Guest. Abbott heard rather than saw him, but the man was speaking as loudly as he could, though 'respectfully' and 'not so much for himself as for the poor workmen and their families', and while he spoke, the crowd was 'perfectly quiet'. It has to be said that Abbott's evidence here does not agree with the depositions collected earlier by the lawyer William Meyrick, which suggested that the crowd was much more volatile and had already begun to push in round the soldiers.

The line of the defence seems to have been twofold here: firstly, that since Lewsyn was speaking in Welsh, which Abbott did not understand, he might just as well have been trying to calm the crowd as urge it to violence; and secondly, that the crowd might not so much have attacked the soldiers as have pressed forward to hear Mr Guest and the anonymous workers' spokesman and so only *seemed* to be attacking. Having dealt with Lewsyn's actions, Sockett now turned to Abbott's testimony with regard to Dic.

> S: Now sir, amongst those persons that you saw wounded, did you see Donald Black?
> A: I did.
> S: I thought you told me that in coming up the steps you did not see him wounded at all.
> A: I did see him wounded on the steps.
> S: But you did not see any wound inflicted upon him before?
> A: No. I saw him struggling with the prisoner Richard Lewis.

Sockett went on then to question Abbott about the behaviour of the crowd, suggesting that the way in which they were pressing forward against the soldiers would inevitably lead to casualties.

> Well now Sir, when the soldiers were wounded and when the poor workmen had felt the effects as you call it of those bayonets, it was at that time (while this had been taking place for some time) that [the soldiers] fired upon them out of the windows.

It would appear that Sockett's defence tactics had some effect, because the junior prosecuting counsel – a Mr Evans – now re-examined Abbott to bring out the points that the crowd was also armed, if only with bludgeons; that the soldiers were holding their weapons in such a way that they could not injure anyone by accident; and that the crowd had advanced deliberately and not because they were being pushed from behind. First of all, however, Abbott was questioned a second time about the precise circumstances of the stabbing.

> E: I understand you to say that you saw Donald Black struggling with Richard Lewis and one or two others.
> A: I am certain there were two.
> E: What did you see Lewis then do? What was the result of that struggle?
> A: Lewis got possession of the musket.
> E: What did he do with the musket?
> A: He stuck the bayonet as it was fixed into the soldier. I looked at him and felt rather indignant at his conduct.
> Mr Sockett (breaking in): Don't tell your feelings.
> A: That made me notice him…

Sockett's interjection here was clearly meant to make Abbott stick to the facts and not indulge in emotional frills that might count against Dic.

Mr Evans then examined William Williams, who was a tailor and a special constable and had been in the passage of the Castle Inn with the other special constables. His evidence made it clear that he could see above the crowd – he could see Lewsyn hanging on the lamp iron – but not below that level. He was a Welsh-speaker and the main purpose of his evidence was to make it clear that Lewsyn's speech was an incitement to attack the soldiers, not an appeal to the crowd to disperse quietly, though he also testified that the crowd had been armed. Dic's name was not mentioned here.

William Rowland, who came next, also spoke mainly about the behaviour of the crowd and Lewsyn's activities. The only reference to Dic was a comment that he had seen both defendants in the crowd at twenty to eleven when the Riot Act was read, which was, of course, before the deputation went into the Castle Inn. He also added that the deputation had been elected by universal suffrage. What exactly that involved is not clear, but presumably it meant that there was some method of selection of suitable candidates, not simply grabbing the ten or twelve men nearest to the door. After Rowland came Thomas Darker, another special constable, who testified that he had seen Dic in the passage coming out with the deputation – i.e. not going out of the front door – and that he had seen him some five or ten minutes later in front of the inn with his hat off, waving it and shouting.

Next was James Drew, also a barber – perhaps Abbott's assistant – who was also questioned by Mr Evans.

> E: Did you see Richard Lewis, the farther one, do anything?
> D: I saw him wrestling with a soldier by the door, and one or
>   two more. I am not quite certain about that.
> E: What did he do?
> D: He pushed the bayonet at his thigh. [Another version says,
>   'in the fleshy part of his thigh'.]

Evans's indication of Dic as 'the farther one' seems to be the nearest to any attempt at identification in the proceedings. J B Bruce Esq. added some details on the arrival and positioning of the soldiers and special constables, and commented that he had not noticed either of the prisoners in the crowd.

Last of all, Donald Black himself gave evidence. His contribution must have been more than a little disappointing for the prosecution if they were expecting a definite identification in the same way that Abbott and Drew had provided. He was questioned by Evans.

> E: Do you know the men who wounded you?
> B: No, sir.
> E. Did you see either of the prisoners in the crowd?
> B: Yes sir. I saw them both.

E: Did you see them doing anything?

B: I did not see them laying hands on anyone.

E: What were they doing?

B: I saw one of the crowd trying to break through our ranks to get in our rear, and Captain Sparks came and turned him back and Lewis Lewis came and said he would not do that to him. [Captain Sparks had apparently found this comment humorous and laughed.]

E: Did you see Richard Lewis do any thing?

B: No, only taking his hat off and cheering and huzzaing, but I did not see him lay hands on anyone.

He also made it clear that when he had seen Dic cheering, this was 'before the rush was made'. According to *The Cambrian* he said, 'I cannot say I saw him stab me. He stood near the place where I was stabbed. I was stabbed on the steps and was taken by James Abbott into the brewhouse.'

At this time it was still not usual to record the defence in any detail other than whatever emerged from the cross-examination of the witnesses. In practice, the defendants must often have been put at a considerable disadvantage by the trial procedure. As explained earlier, they were not allowed to go into the witness box to give evidence, and even their knowledge of the charges against them could be minimal, while their counsel – if they had one – could not sum up for the jury if it was a case of felony, as this was. It was the judge's duty to act as a kind of referee, preventing any major bias, and originally he would cross-question the prosecution witnesses. 'Trial by one's peers' would originally have generally meant trial by those who knew the prisoner and the background, hence the need for the judge to provide balance. In this case, the note on the defence was brief: 'Richard Lewis said on Friday morning this riot began to get up'; after that he left it to his counsel. Lewsyn said nothing. Possibly Sockett made a final statement for the defence, but, as has been said, this would not have been recorded.

According to *The Cambrian*, 'The learned Judge charged the Jury at great length, minutely pointing out every circumstance that made in favour of the prisoners.' At the conclusion he commented, 'The prisoners, being called upon for their defence, leave that to their learned counsel, therefore they don't call witnesses. This case therefore must depend upon the evidence on the part of the prosecution on which you are to form your judgement.' Perhaps he realised Sockett's mistake in relying on the particular line of defence that he had taken. In any case he completed his summing up by pointing out exactly what had to be decided: did Richard Lewis wound Donald Black; did he do so deliberately either in the heat of the moment or without any justifying provocation; and if so, had Lewis Lewis been proved to have been there in order to encourage the commission of that particular act. The jury took about half an hour to consider the evidence and then returned with their verdict. They found Dic guilty, but though they found Lewsyn guilty of encouraging the crowd in general, they had not been satisfied that there was enough evidence to prove 'that Lewis Lewis encouraged the other prisoner Richard Lewis to stab [Donald Black]', so on further consideration, Lewsyn was found not guilty of that offence but guilty of 'rioting'.

At this point in the proceedings Mr Justice Bosanquet, 'with a feeling of humanity towards the prisoners', informed prosecution counsel Mr Maule that 'sufficient proceedings had then taken place relative to the riots at Merthyr, to satisfy the ends of public justice, by the example that would follow these convictions.' No evidence would therefore need to be be offered on the various other indictments: those accused were acquitted – except in a few cases where they had already pleaded guilty, and 'very slight punishments were assigned to them'. Most got twelve months' hard labour, though Joan Jenkins's sons, whom the judge regarded as having been led astray by their mother, got six months apiece. Their mother got twelve months.

Bearing in mind the magnitude of what had happened in Merthyr in early June 1831, this was a quite astonishing turn of events. Effectively, the trials dealt only with the riots, the three days of disorder culminating in the shooting at the Castle Inn, and had almost nothing to say about the events of the following few days – though these, with the workers having managed to keep several bodies of soldiers at bay, must surely have seemed far more threatening as far as the authorities were concerned. One does not have to see *The Cambrian* as an organ of propaganda for the upper classes to realise that the details recorded in it would ensure that the affair was seen as an unfortunate episode of disorder, not a potential forerunner of revolution.

It is worth quoting the final section of *The Cambrian*'s report in full:

> It is to be hoped that the humane and considerate bearing of the Learned Judge towards the prisoners, and the absence of all spirit of vindictiveness on the part of the prosecution will be duly appreciated by the working classes at Merthyr, and will have the effect of inducing those engaged in the riots to reflect with remorse on their past conduct. – They ought to think it particularly fortunate that the lives of two only of their fellow-workmen are thought sufficient to satisfy the demands of the offended laws of their country for offences committed with such violence and ferocity.

Three of the other prisoners had been found guilty of a capital offence and were sentenced to death, but with a recommendation to the mercy of transportation for life. John Phelps was to be transported for 14 years, while John Morgan was also guilty, but had probably saved the life of the man being attacked and was therefore sentenced to 12 months' hard labour. Joan Jenkins and her two sons were guilty of a capital offence, but had admitted their guilt and were sentenced to hard labour. It is quite clear that the trials were symbolic and had far more to do with public opinion in the country as a whole than they did with the crimes and breaches of the peace actually committed in Merthyr.

It is recorded that Bosanquet, when he instructed the jury with regard to the two Lewises, pointed out 'any circumstance that made in favour of the prisoners'. If he did so from the evidence presented during the trial, then he must have had very little to say. Though Sockett, as defence lawyer, did his best to excuse his clients, he seems to have made no attempt to prove them innocent. In Lewsyn's case this was probably inevitable, since his actions had been so public, but in Dic's case there were, as Joseph Tregelles Price soon discovered, numerous witnesses to prove that he was elsewhere at the moment of the stabbing.

In fairness, Sockett clearly did his best to present a case for the defence. Unfortunately he chose to try to build his case on the strict letter of the charge and this proved fatal. The stabbing had certainly occurred, but if it had happened by accident, due to the pressure of the crowd, then there was no case to answer and the crime, as defined in the charge – the deliberate wounding of the soldier – had not been committed. This must have seemed a very sensible defence: in such a crowd, with everyone pushing and being pushed, injuries would have been inevitable. Unfortunately Abbott was quite categorical – he had seen Dic quite deliberately stab Donald Black.

At this point one has to consider the problem of the failure to challenge the identification of Dic as the person who stabbed Black. Surely he should have questioned how the witnesses knew exactly who had carried it out? After all, the space outside the Castle Inn was full of people – perhaps as many as several thousand – all struggling and pushing forward. Was Richard Lewis such an outstanding figure that he could be instantly and convincingly identified in all that confusion? One has to wonder why Sockett made no attempt to challenge Abbott or Drew on their identification. He was said by various people to have defended his clients very ably and this is true as regards the accidental stabbing defence, but on the one vital question he remained silent. Inevitably, one has the impression that for Richard Lewis at least, the trial was simply a formality – his fate was already sealed.

Much of course, depends on Sockett's relationship with his clients. To begin with, he was not just acting for Dic and Lewsyn – he also had all the other Merthyr prisoners to defend. We have no way of knowing whether he had had any real opportunity of discussing the details of their cases with any of his clients, as he would have done in a modern trial, or whether he just had to rely on information provided for him on the day of the hearing. He would not have had access to the depositions gathered by the prosecution or to the names of the witnesses against the prisoners, nor does he seem to have known that there were witnesses who could prove Dic's innocence of the charge against him. Even if he had known, there was little he could have done to bring them to court, as Sydney Smith's comments on the issue demonstrate. Equally, as we have seen, he could not put either of the two Lewises on the stand: defendants had no right to give sworn evidence on their own behalf until 1898. They could 'conduct [their] own defence, cross-examine witnesses and make speeches on [their] own behalf', but this was hardly a practical option for ordinary working men faced with the intricacies of the legal system. We have already seen that the defendants' knowledge of the case against them was severely limited.

From Sockett's point of view, knowing that Dic had been present for at least some of the events outside the Castle Inn, and that Lewsyn had also very publicly been there, demonstrating a lack of malice must have seemed the best defence. The charge against Dic was what would today be one of causing grievous bodily harm – i.e. deliberately causing injury – and that was then a capital charge. If Sockett could establish that any wounding had not been deliberate, then there would be no case to answer. Sadly, even in the unlikely event that he knew that Abbott and Drew were prosecution witnesses, he could have had no idea that they would be so definite in their statements that Dic had quite deliberately stabbed Donald Black. When they did, he must have found himself at a loss as to what to do next. Even if he had known that there were witnesses to Dic's innocence, he could hardly go off in the middle of the trial to look for them. Dic himself seems to have had confidence in Sockett, leaving the defence to him. Yet though he could not go into the witness box, one does have to wonder why Dic chose not to make a statement – or, if it comes to that, why he did not query what Abbott and Drew said. Lewsyn had queried a witness in the previous trial, and as noted above, the defendants were permitted to cross-examine prosecution witnesses. Whatever the reason, the defence's failure at the trial to produce witnesses to Dic's innocence was to prove very damaging, and ultimately fatal. Judge Bosanquet clearly found it very difficult to accept the truth of the witnesses who were later discovered.

The question of witnesses apart, there was certainly something strange about this particular trial. Though both Dic and Lewsyn were accused of the attempted murder of Donald Black, it was clear that Dic was being charged with the actual deed and Lewsyn only with urging him to do so. Both were capital charges and Bosanquet did say in his summing up that if Lewsyn had urged people to attack the soldiers, then he was as guilty as his fellow culprit, 'if not more so', in the attack. Abbott devoted just four sentences to Dic (out of perhaps three and a half pages of testimony): stating categorically that he saw Dic struggling with Donald Black, that he saw him stab the soldier, and that he had not the slightest doubt that it was Dic who had carried out the stabbing. James Drew also testified that he saw Dic struggling with and stabbing Donald Black, though Black himself testified only that he had seen Dic in the crowd cheering. One might have expected Sockett to have cross-questioned Abbott and Drew on this point, but he does not seem to have done so. In fact the matter of identification only seems to have been raised once, when Maule's junior was questioning James Drew and asked, 'Did you see Richard Lewis, the farther one, do anything?'

This raises the question of Abbott's evidence. Joseph Tregelles Price later brought forward quite sufficient witnesses to prove that Dic had not been present when the stabbing took place. It is also highly probable that Abbott had not even been in a position from which he could see who had stabbed Donald Black. We do know that William Meyrick's clerk had altered Abbott's pre-trial deposition:[9] Abbott had originally testified that he was in the passage of the Castle Inn, but this had been changed to 'on the steps of the front door'. The significance of this, of course, was that the passage was full of soldiers, and not somewhere from which he would have been likely to have seen the stabbing, whereas the front steps were where it had happened. In practice this front entrance seems to have been quite modest – three steps up from the pavement and an ordinary-sized front door, not a grand hotel portico. If there were men struggling there, it is doubtful that anyone inside the inn would have been able to see exactly what was happening, even if the passage were not crowded.

Perhaps he did bear a grudge from his earlier confrontation with Dic. Then again, Abbott seems to have been effectively an Englishman in a foreign country and perhaps vulnerable to being pressured by those who wanted an appropriate scapegoat. There is a third alternative: we know today how easy it is to persuade people of the truth of something that never happened. If the person who wounded Donald Black did bear some vague resemblance to Dic, then possibly Abbott, while being interrogated about what he remembered, came to believe that he genuinely had seen Dic wound the soldier.

An old man, interviewed many years later about Dic's funeral, which he had attended, commented that Dic had been executed because 'the masters were afraid of him'. If so, the 'masters' involved were probably not Crawshay or his fellow industrialists – if the verdicts were pre-ordained, then the 'fix' went in at a much more exalted level than Cyfarthfa Castle or Dowlais House. Crawshay may have been a harsh employer and landlord, but he was also something of a radical, interested in reform, and there were many who accused him of encouraging the events of early June. If so, he made at least some amends to those who ended up on trial for their lives, contributing to the defence and allowing his under-manager Henry Kirkhouse to speak in court for Thomas Llewellyn and David Jones. On the evidence we have, Thomas Llewellyn seems far more likely to have been a serious workers' leader than Lewsyn – and as such, possibly someone with whom Crawshay felt he could negotiate, and who was, therefore, worth saving from transportation.

A very much more recent writer, discussing another case of miscarriage of justice, comments that Abbott later said he had lied under oath, being instructed to do so by Lord Melboune.[10] Obviously Lord Melbourne was not involved in the details of the trial, but one has to wonder what part William Meyrick played in the case. Was he instructed to act on behalf of the central authorities? He was responsible for collecting evidence, and according to William Jones, one of the witnesses that Price later discovered, Abbott himself claimed that his evidence had been altered on at least one point. It was William Meyrick, too, who sent an account of the trial to Melbourne. The lawyer had not taken part in the Grand Illumination in May, and he had been treated with hostility in the earlier disturbances of 1816. If Melbourne had already decided that a scapegoat was needed, then Meyrick would have been the right man to ensure that a suitable candidate was found.

Donald Black had been promoted to corporal by the time of the trial, but if this was some sort of bribe to ensure that his evidence was appropriate, then it did not succeed as intended. Then there was the evidence of one of Price's witnesses that Abbott's testimony had been changed. If Dic was – as tradition has it – already known as a fighter for social justice, did Meyrick, in charge of collecting evidence for the prosecution and knowing Dic's reputation, take advantage of that to ensure that the young miner was removed from the scene? Was Isaac Evans right, and did Shoni Crydd, still angry over his dispute with Dic, take advantage of events to get his fellow special constables to arrest his adversary, not expecting events to develop as they did? We know that he did his best to help Lewsyn, who had saved his life, but he stayed on to assist Price with his other petitions too. Was he trying to right a wrong he had caused himself?

Perhaps Bosanquet, who had no clear reason to question the evidence, sensed things were not quite as they seemed. At any rate, his sentencing speech, despite its 'more in sorrow than in anger' tone, showed a kind of muted sympathy for his victims. His particular stress on the well-being of their souls is in sharp contrast to Judge Hardinge in 1801, sentencing condemned men after an earlier riot in Merthyr.

After reporting the sentences handed down to those found guilty, *The Cambrian* commented: 'The prisoners L. and R. Lewis, on their trials, manifested great firmness of demeanour, and did not seem to feel their awful situation, but during the time their sentences were pronounced, they showed the greatest mental distress, and at the conclusion they cried out and groaned in inexpressible agony.'[11] In Lewsyn's case, this may have been because he thought he had secured some sort of deal in the previous trial which had now been cancelled. For Dic, one suspects, it was the shock of learning that innocence was irrelevant. Throughout his trial he had remained calm, confident that justice would not fail the innocent; now he knew that justice was at best fallible, at worst corrupt. What one senses in the accounts of his last hours is not fear, but an intense anger.

CHAPTER 5

Last Days

ONCE THE TRIAL was over, the condemned men were taken back to their cells in Cardiff Gaol. For Lewsyn there must have been still the hint of a future. He had been found not guilty of the major charge in the joint trial over the stabbing of Donald Black, and though he still faced a death sentence from the earlier trial, those convicted then had been recommended to mercy, i.e. transportation. However, Judge Bosanquet, in his summing up, made it clear that Lewsyn's actions in leading the mob and in being armed, both on the day of the shooting and afterwards, set him apart from the others, and though the judge had looked very carefully through the evidence, he could find nothing that would allow him, in this case, to recommend the culprit to mercy.

And yet both men had shown signs of distress as Bosanquet spoke, and cried out in shock when the sentence was announced. For Dic, knowing himself to be innocent, the reaction is understandable, even if it had been naïve to expect the truth to save him. For Lewsyn, one has to wonder. There have always been rumours – that he was saved because he was the illegitimate son of a local grandee, or even that he had been in some way working with the authorities, perhaps as an *agent provocateur*. Neither seems likely, though his words after the execution, 'Indeed he [Dic] didn't do it. No, indeed, I know who did it, but I will never tell anyone,' are curious. He could not have gone into the witness box in his own defence, but he could have spoken up for Dic without necessarily identifying the actual culprit.

The execution was set for Saturday, 30 July, giving the two men a fortnight in which to prepare themselves for their end. Bosanquet, in a tone more in sorrow than anger, had recommended that they examine their consciences and ask for forgiveness for their crimes, and had promised that they would have a minister of the Gospel with them to help them with this.[1] There was, of course, a prison chaplain, several Nonconformist ministers visited and Dic may well have also had his brother-in-law to support him. Morgan Howells kept a diary which listed his preaching engagements, crossing them off as they were completed. In the week beginning 13 August he should have been on a preaching tour in the Brecon area, but these dates are not crossed off.[2] Family tradition suggests that Howells, seeing that all other efforts had failed, went to London to ask the King for a pardon, but without success, and did not get back in time for the execution. If that was the case and he was elsewhere, perhaps that explains the arrival of the other four ministers.

Meanwhile, up in Merthyr Tydfil, Taliesin Williams and others had begun to organise a petition asking for a reprieve for Dic and Lewsyn. Petitions of this kind were a regular event, for both those sentenced to death and those sentenced to transportation. In 1829 some 1,278 petitions were received by the Home Secretary, about a third of them for those sentenced to death.[3] The Merthyr petition was apparently presented to Lord Melbourne himself by Henry and William Morgan and included some eleven thousand signatures, according to *The Cambrian*, though that seems an unlikely total even allowing that the Merthyr area was the most heavily populated urban part of Wales at the time. The document itself has disappeared, but it did not include any of the evidence that Joseph Tregelles Price was to uncover. This lack, together with the inclusion of a statement supposedly by Dic and Lewsyn in which they admitted their guilt, was to prove a major error, since it mitigated against the evidence of Price's newly discovered witnesses when that was presented later. The two Lewises apparently knew nothing about the petition or the statement. If they were ever told about them, they were certainly not involved in drafting them.

For us, of course, with the benefit of hindsight and of Price's patient collection of evidence, the innocence of Richard Lewis seems clear, but in July and August 1831 that was by no means the case. For many people, then and now, the verdict of a court is sacrosanct and not to be questioned. In the circumstances, one can understand why the Merthyr petitioners thought it would be better to admit guilt but express contrition than to insist on innocence – and of course Lewsyn actually had done what he was accused of, in urging on the mob and carrying arms. The excuse for his reprieve, when it came, was for something else.

As it happens, there is a much more recent example of this assumption of guilt in Nicholas Cooke's 2003 article on the trial. In *The Legal History of Wales*, T G Watkins comments that this article 'provides a substantial reassessment of the status of Dic Penderyn as an innocent working class martyr through examining transcripts of the trial from the viewpoint of a forensic advocate.' Cooke's final verdict was that Dic was guilty of the crime of which he was accused. However, it would appear that he either did not know of, or had not read, Price's two petitions.[4]

In the first week after the verdict had been delivered and sentence passed, the two men had nothing to do but consider their fate and what had led them to it. Whether they were allowed visits from family or friends is not recorded, but Bosanquet's promise of religious support seems to have been more than amply fulfilled. The prison chaplain, Daniel Jones, was regularly there, there were four Wesleyan ministers who were there on the last two days of Dic's life, and we know of at least two others – William Jones, a Baptist minister, and Lewis Powell, an Independent – who were there on 1 August, when they witnessed affidavits from Lewsyn and Dic.

Lewsyn's affidavit raises a serious question. Both documents are very brief: Lewsyn denied having known Dic before they were both in Cardiff Gaol, while Dic, in his own affidavit, denied having been involved in the wounding of Donald Black. But why was Lewsyn so concerned to deny that he had known Dic before they were taken to Cardiff Gaol? Although they had had a joint trial, the charges were distinct, and though Lewsyn's actions could have been said to have enabled the stabbing, there was no suggestion of conspiracy to wound. Tradition certainly held that the two men were connected, either through family or friendship, but even if they had been brothers, as was sometimes suggested, that would have had no bearing on the legal case. And by 1 August, Lewsyn had been reprieved and was waiting to be removed to the hulks. One gets the impression that even at this late date, Lewsyn felt that just knowing Dic was dangerous.

Meanwhile up in Merthyr, James Abbott was suffering major harassment. People burst into his shop and dragged customers outside, so others were afraid to go there and his takings dropped to nothing, and "Murderer!" was shouted at him in the street. He was apparently in constant fear – though in practice no one seems to have actually laid hands on him.[5] He appealed to the authorities for help, and perhaps their response was enough to prevent any serious physical attack on him. At any rate, he evidently remained in Merthyr and in business because the illustration of *c.*1844 shows Abbott's barber's shop next door to the Castle Inn, with a white-aproned figure (Abbott himself?) standing in the doorway.

Once the trial was over, Bosanquet had continued on the Assize circuit, but the business at Merthyr continued to occupy his mind. The days of the Bloody Code of earlier decades, when children could be hanged for stealing a crust, were over by now, but the death penalty was still in active operation – in theory, if not always in fact. Of the non-Merthyr Rising defendants at the July Assizes in Cardiff, five were sentenced to death but reprieved on the spot, in favour of transportation. Transportation, of course, solved two problems: it removed the criminal and helped to provide new blood for the growing Australian colony. In those circumstances, presiding over an actual death sentence – one that was to be carried out – may well have been relatively unusual. And Bosanquet soon had further reasons for considering the matter of the two condemned Merthyr rioters.

Joseph Tregelles Price (1784–1854) was a Quaker ironmaster from Neath Abbey.[6] The Price family came originally from Cornwall; Peter and Anna Price, Joseph Tregelles Price's parents, were noted for their charitable works and were active Quakers. Joseph himself was also active locally, among other things establishing a works school at the Neath Abbey Ironworks. He was a member of the Anti-Slavery Movement, and one of the founders of the Peace Society in London, ordering that no cannon or other weapons of war were to be made at his works. Quite why he decided to interest himself in the case of the two Lewises we do not know – he does not seem to have been in the habit of visiting condemned men, and though he had a book on the death penalty in his library, that may have been acquired later. There is a possible link via Aberafan. John Reynolds, the builder of the famous aqueduct at Pontrhydyfen, was a Quaker and his former partner, Robert Smith, proprietor of the Margam Tinplate Works, was a committed Methodist and a deacon at Carmel Calvinistic Methodist Chapel, Aberafan. Dic's family were local, very possibly members at Carmel, and his name may perhaps have come up in conversation at a meeting of local industrialists, who would naturally have been concerned about events in Merthyr. This can only be a hypothesis, but it is worth recording. However it happened, Price's interest was sparked, and although he was anxious for both men, his main effort was for Dic.

The story of the events at Merthyr and the fate of those found guilty was common knowledge. Whatever did spark Price's interest in the affair, on Sunday 24 July, just under a week before the date of the execution, he visited the two Lewises in Cardiff Gaol.[7] In Price's first petition on behalf of Richard Lewis he explains that the man was wholly unknown to him until he visited him on the 24th, but Dic's narration was evidently so convincing that Price felt he must make enquiries to see whether there was anything to back up the statement. He set off for Merthyr immediately – time was already running out for Dic – and there proceeded to look for witnesses and question them, though without giving any hint of what Dic had told him. At some point, presumably after he got to Merthyr, he was joined in his search by John Thomas, 'a constable' better known locally as Shoni Crydd, who was particularly anxious to help Lewsyn. It is possible that Thomas had already been working on this – Bosanquet knew that Lewsyn had saved the special constable's life as early as 21 July, before Price became involved, though how he had heard this remains unclear.

When Price spoke to him, Dic told his visitor that he had not been at the front of the Castle Inn after coming out from the deputation. When he heard the firing, he and others ran off towards the Iron Bridge, and he named two women who could bear witness to that. Then Price asked him if he had ever had any quarrel with James Abbott, and Dic told him how there had been a confrontation between them on the evening of the Illumination, about a month before the riots. Dic said that William John David had been there and could bear witness to the event. Once in Merthyr, Price interviewed the two women Dic had named, and he also spoke to two other witnesses – one of whom, as well as confirming that Dic had been at the back of the Castle Inn, gave a description of Dic's clothing on the day. Price also interviewed three others. One, David Abraham, a special constable, had been standing near Abbott, had cautioned Dic (earlier?) against 'going forward', and did not believe he was in the crowd at the time of the stabbing. Two others had witnessed the stabbing and were quite sure that the man responsible was dressed in 'a drab coloured' coat, not one that was blue or black, as were the clothes that Dic was wearing. Price added that there were others ready to offer testimony, but since time was pressing, he had decided to head for London to put his evidence in front of the proper authorities.

Price presented his findings in the form of two petitions: one for Dic, one for Lewsyn. The latter admitted that he had been part of the mob outside the Castle Inn, but stressed that 'he did not say a word to encourage the men in the mob to seize the soldiers' arms' and that someone else had taken his place on the lamp iron, egging the crowd on. He claimed that there were 'a score of men' who could testify to the truth of this statement. One has to suspect that Lewsyn here was just trying desperately and understandably to avoid execution. At any rate, Price does not appear to have looked for the witnesses that Lewsyn claimed could speak for him. The main argument of the petition for Lewsyn was that Lewsyn had saved John Thomas (a.k.a. Shoni Crydd)'s life, at the risk of his own, when the crowd had wanted to kill Thomas outside Joseph Coffin's house. John Thomas confirmed this and even accompanied Price to London 'under a feeling of anxiety and duty to save the life of Lewis Lewis'. Whether Thomas also helped Price with his search for witnesses to confirm Dic's story is not stated, but according to a much later report, Dic's arrest was due to John Thomas. He and Dic had had a fight, which made the special constables 'suspicious' of Dic, so they went to arrest him while they were rounding up the rioters.[8] If this was the case, then Dic's plight was due to Thomas even more than to Abbott and Drew, but although Price mentions that Thomas was with him when he was looking for witnesses, there is no evidence that the special constable made any particular effort to save Dic.

Price was in London by 27 July. He was staying at Hatchet's Hotel in Piccadilly, where he wrote out his two petitions, for Lewsyn and for Dic, addressing them formally to William IV. However, the person he really needed to see was the Home Secretary, Lord Melbourne. Initially Price wanted to gain a stay of execution so that the case could be looked at again by Bosanquet, in the hope of causing the judge to change his mind and recommend a reprieve. According to *The Cambrian*, Price's first efforts got nowhere, largely due to the effect of the Merthyr petition, which had merely confirmed Bosanquet's opinion. Though *The Cambrian* does not say so, there was also generally a certain amount of doubt about petitions – a suggestion that new evidence might have been concocted in the hope of saving the condemned person, However, Price was not a man to be easily defeated. He had the support, it seems, of the County and Borough MPs for Glamorgan and Cardiff, C R M Talbot[9] of Margam and Lord James Crichton Stuart, younger brother of Lord Bute, and most likely through their efforts he was able to put his petitions before Lord Brougham, the Lord Chancellor. This latter official immediately took up the cause and Price was able to make a personal application to Lord Melbourne for at least a brief meeting.

By now, of course, time was running out: the executions were due on the 30th, and this was late in the evening of the 28th. The Home Secretary was in the House of Lords, but came out and Price was able to lay out his case and 'exhibit' John Thomas as concrete evidence. Melbourne then granted a respite until 13 August, promising to send the new information to Bosanquet, who was then at Brecon, for his consideration.[10] This must have seemed very encouraging and Price continued his efforts, going by way of Cardiff and Merthyr to Brecon, to speak to Bosanquet. He got there by 2 August.

Even before Price had begun to gather evidence and travel between Wales and London, Bosanquet had begun a correspondence about the case with Lord Melbourne. He wrote first, at some length, as early as 17 July, chiefly concerning Lewsyn. Bosanquet explained that Lewsyn had been found guilty, with others, of robbery and that the others had been recommended to mercy, but not Lewsyn because he had been a leading figure in the riots and had later been seen carrying arms. He had also been indicted as an accomplice in Dic's crime of stabbing the soldier, though he had been acquitted of this. Dic is only mentioned in passing. Bosanquet does not, at this point, recommend that Lewsyn should be reprieved – if anything he is justifying his decision not to recommend the man to mercy – but the case was obviously occupying his thoughts.

He wrote again on 21 July, once again chiefly concerning Lewsyn. He now doubted the propriety of carrying out the execution given that he had discovered that Lewsyn had saved the life of one of the special constables, John Thomas, when he was attacked by the mob. Bosanquet therefore proposed sending an order for a stay of execution for a week, on the next Saturday or Sunday (23 or 24 July), following this a few days later with a reprieve, subject to Melbourne's agreement.

The next letter in the series, dated the 29th, was from Melbourne, informing Bosanquet that Price had been in touch with him, offering evidence that Dic was not guilty. Melbourne had not 'seen any authentic report of the evidence given at the trial', so he was sending Price's petition to the judge to see whether in his opinion it offered any reason for altering his view of Dic's guilt. In the meantime he had granted a fortnight's respite, but had directed that the prisoner was to be told that this was only for the purpose of checking Price's statement. Clearly he was concerned not to raise any false hopes.

On 30 July Bosanquet wrote to confirm that he had sent a reprieve for Lewsyn, altering his sentence to one of transportation for life. Whether Lewsyn had had any hint of this we do not know, but on 1 August he and Dic made solemn affidavits witnessed by Daniel Jones, the chaplain of the gaol, and two ministers: William Jones, a Baptist, and Lewis Powell, an Independent. The draft document is very brief: 'Lewis Lewis has sworn solemnly that he did not know Richard Lewis until they became prisoners in Cardiff. Richard Lewis has solemnly denied having any part in wounding the soldier. August 1 1831.' The fuller version, also signed by the chaplain and the two ministers, states: 'We hereby humbly Certify that we have respectively attended Richard Lewis, now under sentence of death in the Gaol of this place since his conviction, and that he has uniformly and solemnly denied any participation in, or knowledge of, the act of wounding, or endeavouring to wound the Soldier, for which offence the said Richard Lewis is condemned to die.' This statement was followed on the same document by another, this time by James Lewis, who was the surgeon at the gaol. He wrote: 'Richard Lewis has continued uniformly to deny the act of wounding the Soldier or carrying arms', adding, 'This has been voluntary on his part & not arising from any examination from me' and 'Lewis Lewis has also volunteered in the most sacred manner previous to & since his condemnation stated that he had no knowledge of Richard Lewis until they became prisoners in this Gaol.'

Also on 1 August, Bosanquet wrote again to Melbourne, sending a copy of the witness statements collected by William Meyrick. It is not clear whether this was, like *The Cambrian*'s account, a record of the trial itself; it is very similar to the official record, but not identical. As it gives only the words of the witnesses and not the questions they were being asked, it is sometimes a little confusing, and (as mentioned earlier) the only note as to the defence is: 'Richard Lewis said on Friday morning this riot began to get up'; after that he apparently left his defence to his counsel, while Lewsyn said nothing.

Perhaps the official shorthand record of the trial had not yet been transcribed, but if this was Melbourne's main evidence as regards the business, then it was not altogether helpful.

Bosanquet also sent Price's petition, which he had now had an opportunity to read. He raised the obvious query – if Dic had in fact not been in the crowd outside the Castle Inn at the time of the stabbing, why had this not been mentioned at the trial? Nor had this been suggested in the petitions on behalf of Lewsyn and Dic earlier presented to Melbourne (these were presumably the petition(s) presented by Taliesin Williams and his group), which had apparently been shown to Bosanquet before being sent to London. The judge also queried the sudden remembering of the scuffle between Dic and James Abbott, and said finally that even if Dic *was* at the back of the Castle Inn before the firing started, and a man in a 'coat of drab colour' had been seen stabbing a soldier, that did not make the evidence given in the trial untrue. He made no recommendation, either to mercy or to death.

While Bosanquet was clearly justified in asking why no one had mentioned at the trial that Dic was elsewhere at the crucial moment, his dismissal of Price's evidence could be seen as a refusal to admit a mistake on his part. After all, if an innocent man had somehow been condemned to death in error, that suggested a major failure in the legal process. Price himself arrived at Brecon the next day, having come via Cardiff and Merthyr, and brought with him the affidavit that Dic and Lewsyn had made the day before. The judge duly forwarded this to the Home Office by the hand of Lord James Crichton Stuart. How soon this reached Melbourne, if it did, is not known, but on 4 August the Home Secretary wrote to both Bosanquet and Price to say that there would be no further respite: the execution would take place on 13 August.

Price had not given up. His first petition had failed, but he had gone back to Merthyr to look for more witnesses, and he now presented a second petition to Bosanquet. We know that the judge had queried Dic's apparently sudden remembrance of the scuffle with Abbot, so this time Price concentrated on evidence on that subject, on undermining the validity of Abbott's statement, and on offering evidence about the man who *had* stabbed Donald Black. He had found some 13 new witnesses and also interviewed Abbott himself. Two men, William John David and Edward Matthews, who had been in the street near the Bush Inn on the night of the Illumination, said that they had seen Abbott strike Dic; while David Rees, who was a miner but also a Baptist lay preacher, said he had heard Abbott threaten Dic. Abbott himself said he did not know Dic, had never had a quarrel with him and had not even seen him before the events at the Castle Inn. He produced three witnesses to say that he had not been near the Bush Inn in May anyway – though one of them commented that Abbott *might* have been there without his seeing him.

Price then turned to the confrontation outside the Castle Inn. One Mr Marsden, 'a respectable linen draper of Merthyr', said he had seen Dic leave the Castle Inn by the back door; the wife of James Rice, who lived opposite the inn, witnessed that Dic was wearing a blue jacket and trousers, and though she had seen him there before he went into the Castle Inn, she had not seen him after the deputation came out. William Jones, a fitter at the Cyfarthfa Works, said he had been in the lawyer William Meyrick's office on the Thursday before the Quarter Sessions began. James Abbott had been there, listening while the evidence he had given was read back to him, and had told Meyrick's clerk, a Mr Davis, that this had been recorded incorrectly, because he, Abbott, had been in the passage of the inn, not on the front steps at the crucial moment. Jones added that he considered that it would have been impossible for anyone in the passage 'thronged as it was by the soldiers in the front' to have seen a stabbing outside the building. The transcript of evidence taken by Meyrick and sent to Melbourne gives Abbott as saying 'I was ordered to take my station in the passage. I was ordered to take care of the soldiers outside', which while not actually placing him on the steps suggests that he was closer to what was happening there than he really was.

Next William Edwards, Master Collier and 'undertaker of job work in those departments at Penydarren Ironworks', gave evidence that he was with James Drew in the passage of the Castle Inn several yards from the front door, and it was impossible for either of them to have seen what was happening outside. He and Drew stayed together for about 20 minutes after the firing was over, at which point Drew went off to let his wife know that he was safe. He was away for just under an hour, after which he rejoined Edwards and they spent several hours in a nearby public house, during which time Drew never mentioned having seen Dic stab Donald Black. Price added a note that those who had seen a soldier stabbed had seen a man in a drab smock do the deed and they thought he had been killed in the fighting. He ended by saying that in view of this new evidence, which at the very least suggested that the case was not as clear-cut as it had seemed, he was asking for a reprieve. Price had clearly this time looked not just for evidence, but for specific statements to counter the prosecution's case.

If his witnesses were telling the truth, then Abbott and Drew were lying, and the account of the 1 May confrontation between Abbott and Dic would obviously be helpful to suggest a reason for this. It could hardly even have been a matter of confusion, because some of the new witnesses had actually seen what happened, knew Dic and were ready to swear that the culprit was not even dressed in similar clothes. Since these witnesses included shopkeepers, a special constable, 'a Gentleman residing in Merthyr' – persons of some weight in the community, not simply ordinary workmen – and others who were clearly not part of the mob, it is unlikely that they had for any reason colluded to provide false information.

Bosanquet, having read the new petition, sent it on to Melbourne – writing from Hay on 4 August, in a letter that crossed with Melbourne's – to say that though he could still not quite accept that the trial evidence was wrong, Price's evident sincerity and care in collecting material had made a strong impression on him. It might therefore be sensible to issue a reprieve. He added that there appeared to be a strong feeling of doubt in Merthyr about the justice of the case. The circumstances of the riot outside the Castle Inn were so confused that it was probably impossible to get at the truth of the matter. He noted too that the Taliesin Williams petition, which had acknowledged guilt, had not been authorised by or even made known to Dic and Lewsyn, and that Dic's affidavit had earlier been forwarded to Melbourne.

Bosanquet received Melbourne's letter of 4 August two days later, on the 6th, and wrote again on the 7th to confirm that he had sent Price's second petition to London, together with his own thoughts on the case. If it was thought fit to recommend a reprieve, he added, then, as with Lewsyn, Dic should be removed from Cardiff as soon as possible. That was the end of the correspondence.

One has to wonder why Bosanquet took so much convincing. Melbourne is understandable: there was a perceived need to stamp down hard on movements of discontent – a scapegoat had to be found. And, of course, there had to be something to balance the death toll at the Castle Inn – higher than that at Peterloo a few years before. But though the second, stronger petition was sent to him, we do not know if he received or read it. Bosanquet seems to have had doubts about its arrival, hence his letter of 7 August. The judge is more of a problem. He was very impressed by Price and must have realised that if Price's evidence was true, then Dic could not have wounded Donald Black. It was not simply that Dic was not in the crowd in front of the inn at the time of the wounding; there were witnesses who identified someone dressed differently to Dic as the culprit, and others who stated that Drew and Abbott could not have seen what they had sworn to. Certainly Price's first set of witnesses could have been seen as friends of Dic's who wanted to save him and might be manipulating their evidence, something which was not unheard of in appeals, but those in the second petition were varied enough to be genuine. In fairness to Bosanquet, he clearly had a respect for the law and found it very difficult both as a lawyer and as a human being to accept that the process had gone wrong in this case. Despite the evidence that Price gathered together, Bosanquet never quite admitted that the verdict had been wrong, only that 'the justice of it will be considered doubtful'.

By the time Price began his search for evidence to help Dic and Lewsyn, the latter was clearly already part way to a reprieve, but no one seems to have made that known to Price. Perhaps the message had not yet reached Cardiff – Bosanquet had said he would send it on the 23rd or 24th, but there were still several days before the execution date and the messenger may not have hurried. The grounds for the reprieve, which was sent on 30 July, were clear – the others found guilty with Lewsyn in the earlier trials had been recommended to mercy and though it was plain that Lewsyn had been involved in more than just the actual rioting, this had not been one of the charges against him and he had been found not guilty in the wounding trial. Legally, therefore, a reprieve was justified. Despite the conspiracy suspected by public opinion, it all seems straightforward enough.

Whether Dic knew that Lewsyn had been reprieved is unknown. If he did, then it must have been particularly painful to see the date for his own execution coming nearer. We know little or nothing about what happened to him in those last few weeks. He had already prepared himself once for death, on the original date for the execution: his coffin had been provided and his grave dug, 'the Deputy Sheriff and his officers were in attendance' and even a hangman had been obtained.[11] The authorities had evidently had trouble finding one – quite why is another puzzle. Certainly there were fewer executions by the beginning of the nineteenth century, but they were hardly unknown. *The Cambrian* stated that though Gloucester, Bristol and Ilchester had been searched, no qualified person had been found who was willing to carry out the hanging, and finally the authorities had had to fall back on a novice from London, whose poverty was such that the hangman's fee had persuaded him to do the job. *The Cambrian* does not suggest that there were no hangmen available, but rather that not one of them was willing to officiate.

The stay of execution that Price had managed to obtain for Dic was almost too late. Melbourne agreed to it on the Thursday evening and someone must have ridden non-stop to Cardiff in time to halt proceedings before early Saturday morning. The traumatic circumstances of this last-minute postponement cannot have been eased by Melbourne's insistence that Dic should be told that the respite was given only 'for the purpose of enquiring into the facts alleged in the statement received from Mr. Price', and not, as happened in Lewsyn's case, as the preliminary to a reprieve. In other words, Price and his two supporters, C R M Talbot and Lord James Crichton Stuart, were too important to be simply ignored, but Melbourne had already decided that the execution would go ahead on the 13th. Price's evidence and Bosanquet's doubts were irrelevant. The last official word seems to have come from Lord Brougham, in a note that mixed a life-or-death decision with mundane housekeeping, saying. 'I have looked at the papers and have no doubt the law should take its course. Bank cheque – it can't be anywhere to be found. I am sure it never came. H.B.'

Whether Dic appreciated the attentions of the various clergymen who had been sent to help him prepare for eternity, we cannot know. It is likely that one of these was his brother-in-law, Morgan Howells, and it is possible that Dic's wife was able to visit him. One of the stories attached to these days says that Elizabeth was either pregnant or had just given birth and that as a result of her having to walk down to Cardiff from Merthyr, her baby died. There was in fact a baptism of a child, Mary Lewis, daughter of Richard and Elizabeth Lewis, on 26 July.[12] The ceremony was registered in the nearby St John's Church, but seems to have happened in the gaol itself and the child's father was noted as 'convict'. Although the baby did not die then, she lived for less than two years after that, being buried on 16 March 1833.

By Thursday, 11 August it was clear to Dic that there would be no reprieve. He wrote or dictated a note to his sister Elizabeth to ask her to arrange for his body to be collected and taken for burial, saying she was to ask Philip Lewis to come down 'tonight' with a cart and 'as many men as he can'. The message reached Aberafan on the Thursday afternoon, and the old man whose account was later given in *Y Drysorfa* described what happened: 'the news ran like wildfire through the neighbourhood ... they stopped working there, and everybody who was in the field went sorrowfully towards their homes.' On the Friday the farmers gathered together to go to Cardiff. It would seem that people came from a wide area, not just from Aberafan, because in the end there were more than 30 gambos (haycarts) and hundreds of men on foot making their way towards Cardiff, which they reached at about six o'clock on the Saturday morning. Among them was a young boy whose memories of the event were recorded many years later in *Y Drysorfa*.[13]

Meanwhile Dic had also, it seems, written to his wife. She was in Cardiff but perhaps not allowed visiting rights until the very end. On the Friday morning he was visited by two Wesleyan Methodist ministers, Edmund Evans and David Williams. Evans later spoke of the events of the Friday and Saturday morning, and also recorded them in his diary.[14] These ministers were strangers to Dic and seem to have accepted his guilt, and also seem to have viewed him as someone with no religious background. Evans commented that they 'had exhorted him to ask "for Jesus sake", for he had no idea of the Intercessor' – this of the brother-in-law of Morgan Howells and product of the Sunday School! It has to be said that their reports show a certain degree of self-admiration at their own noble performance as spiritual advisers, but they do allow us to hear Dic's own voice, briefly but clearly.

> Mr. Williams asked the condemned man some questions about the matter of his soul. Then [Dic] said that he hoped that God would have pity on him and would show in some way that he was not guilty of stabbing the soldier. "Richard *bach*," said Mr. Williams, "I am not asking anything about that. I wish to be honest with you, because you are going to face the all-knowing God and it would be a terrible thing for you to meet him with a lie on your lips." "Indeed it would," he said then, "But I am not guilty."

In the afternoon the two other ministers, Messrs Jones and Rowlands, also went to pray with him.

On the Saturday morning two of the ministers, Williams and Jones, arrived at the gaol at 6 a.m., to find Dic and the prison chaplain, the Revd Daniel Jones, deep in prayer. There then seems to have been a relay of prayers until the other two, Evans and Rowlands, joined them an hour later. At that point the gaoler arrived with the condemned man's last meal, a cup of tea and a thin slice of bread and butter. Dic drank the tea but left the bread, and then his wife came to say goodbye to him – in a cell full of clergymen who do not appear to have had the common sense to give them a last few minutes of privacy. After that the company moved to the prison chapel where they all, including Dic, took communion. Then the clock struck eight and the final act began.

The group went out into the courtyard, where the executioner and the keeper of the gaol came forward, tying Dic's arms and putting fetters on his hands. Then a little procession formed: first the sheriff and the keeper, then the chaplain, who was reading the burial service; next came Dic between the executioner and Mr Williams, and finally the other three ministers. They mounted the scaffold, which was outside Cardiff Gaol on St Mary's Street, to see thousands of spectators in front of them. These may have included Dic's brother and sister, Matthew and Sarah.

As the hangman placed the rope around his neck, Dic cried out for the last time, "*Arglwydd, dyma gamwedd!*" (Lord, here is injustice!) and then, more quietly, 'O Jesus, forgive them and me.' The trap opened and he fell. This time they had found an executioner in Worcester, who was, one hopes, less of a novice, but Dic's foot caught – kicking out in a final protest? – and after two minutes the hangman had to pull on his feet to finish the job.[15] The body was left to hang until 9 a.m. (at which point and not when he fell, there *was* a thunderstorm and heavy rain). In later years, men who had been schoolboys in 1831 remembered seeing the body hanging as they went to school. At nine o'clock it was taken down and handed over to the family, who took it to the Prince Regent Inn in Crockherbtown (now Queen Street). There they placed it in a more suitable coffin, using the prison box as an inner shell.

Morgan Howells had been asked to preach a suitable moral sermon under the gallows, but not surprisingly, he refused. According to family tradition, he had gone off in a desperate attempt to persuade the King to grant a reprieve. Whether he ever had an audience with William IV is not recorded, but if so, he was unsuccessful. It is likely, therefore, that his absence was the reason for the delay in setting off for Aberafan: the funeral party was waiting for him to return – something which can hardly have pleased the authorities, who were anxious to have the whole affair put well out of the way.

The mourners started for Aberafan at about 6 o'clock on Sunday morning.[16] Their first stop was at St Nicholas, the first village on the road west across the Vale, where a crowd had come from Cowbridge to meet them. At Cowbridge, where the mourners were offered bread and cheese, they were joined by another crowd, from Bridgend, and at Bridgend by still more, from Pyle. Finally at Pyle, the Aberafan contingent were waiting. This incremental increase may be the origin of the story that the body was refused burial at every church until they reached Aberafan – which was, of course, always the actual destination. The crowd was too large to fit into the old St Mary's church, and so the burial service was held at the graveside, with the curate, E W Thomas, officiating as usual. He recorded the death in the parish register: Dic's grave was near the churchyard wall, with six graves between it and the boundary. Felon or not, he was buried in consecrated ground. When the curate had finished, Morgan Howells jumped up onto the wall and began to preach. We only have the first two sentences of what he said, but even in those it is impossible not to hear the affection and pride that Dic's brother-in-law felt. 'Dic *bach*,' he said, 'are you there? You were not afraid of the rope.' Even the anonymous correspondent who provided a second, less favourable account of the hanging in *The Cambrian* had noted Dic's firm bearing in those last few minutes.

Meanwhile, back in Cardiff, the four ministers and the chaplain had been making their way out by way of the chapel when they heard Lewsyn crying out in anguish, 'saying many times, "Indeed he didn't do it," meaning the wounding of the soldier, "no, indeed I know who did do it; but I will never tell anyone."'[17] *The Cambrian* had a fuller version of this: 'Richard is innocent, for I know him not to have been there. I was by the soldier. If I had been sharing the same fate, I would have disclosed it on the scaffold.'[18] *The Cambrian* made no direct comment on this, but went on to say: 'It is most particularly worthy of remark that Richard, the day before his execution, being urged to make a full confession as all hopes of mercy were gone, replied, "One way to obtain mercy is to <u>speak the truth</u>, and in asserting my innocence, <u>I do speak the truth</u>."'

The Cambrian did not report the funeral or the procession across the Vale, and we do not know who took part in it apart from the farmers of the area. Was there a contingent from Merthyr? The impression that one gets is that the population of that town was, for the moment – very understandably – keeping its head well down. They were still under military control, with a garrison left in the town in case of any further trouble, not to mention the discouraging effect of the trials and sentences. In the end, there are more questions than answers when we come to look at the response of the general public to the events of 1831. For instance, we are told that on the day of Dic's execution the shops in Cardiff were closed and many of the respectable inhabitants left the town. Was this because they feared the rowdiness that had accompanied executions in the Georgian era, or were they expressing silent disapproval of the death sentence?

Back in Aberafan, the curate had recorded the burial in the register of deaths as usual. "Richard Lewis, Merthyr Tydfil, 14 Aug. 1831, 23 years. E W Thomas, Curate." Then he added a note: 'The unfortunate man was executed at Cardiff on the 13th August 1831, for stabbing Donald Black, one of the 93rd Highlanders, whilst stationed on duty at Merthyr during the riots on the 3 June last. He was indicted under 9 Geo. IV, Cap. 31 and 12.'[19] While one can understand why the curate might have wanted to note what was clearly a remarkable event, one wonders why he felt it necessary to add the detail of the charge. Although the penal code was less bloody by 1831, the charge was still technically one carrying a capital sentence – yet though his injury was no doubt painful, Donald Black had not been seriously wounded. The Revd Thomas would not have been the only one to query the matter – indeed, as noted, it has often been taken for granted that Donald Black must have been killed.

CHAPTER 6

Aftermath

THE AUTHORITIES WERE no doubt hoping that the unfortunate business was now over and done with, buried in the grave along with their victim. Still, they must have been aware that not everyone was convinced that justice had been done, and *The Cambrian* did show some evidence of official unease. To begin with, they published two accounts of the execution: one presumably by their own correspondent, relatively favourable to Dic; the other, anonymous, account much less so.[1]

The readership of *The Cambrian* would have been mostly among those groups – industrialists, gentry, professional men, shopkeepers and the like – who saw themselves as possible victims of any violence, and the newspaper was therefore unlikely to be sympathetic to those on trial. However, by the time of the execution, they had come to hope that Dic would be reprieved, and their account stresses his prayerfulness in the hours before his death and his protestations of innocence even on the scaffold. 'He ascended the platform with a firm step ... declaring as he walked up the ladder, "I am going to suffer unjustly. God, who knows all things, knows it is so."' As has been noted, they report Lewsyn's words afterwards, and his agony of mind at what had happened to Dic. They also talk of the latter's insistence that he was telling the truth, though 'at the same time he freely admitted his criminality in participating in the wicked and riotous proceedings at

Merthyr, but evidently considered himself unjustly treated in being singled out as the solitary victim, when so many were at least equally guilty.' This may have been a misunderstanding by *The Cambrian* of the regret for past sins noted by the ministers. If he *had* been involved in either the earlier rioting or the activities after the confrontation outside the Castle Inn, it is strange that no one mentioned this at any point.

Curiously, *The Cambrian*'s report ends with: 'It will be remembered that the alleged crime for which he suffered was "stabbing Donald Black ... at Merthyr on the 3rd of June."' The underlining in the report would suggest that *The Cambrian* had doubts about the justice of the proceedings, but that the writer perhaps felt that stating this too openly would not have pleased either the newspaper's readers or the authorities.

However, immediately following its own straightforward report of the execution, with its stress on Dic's religious devotions, the paper printed what it headlined as 'Another Account'. The purpose of this version was quite clearly to assert his guilt. 'In the interval between his commitment and trial, the behaviour of this unhappy man was remarkably cool and composed. His explanation of his conduct at that time was that he conceived himself to be in a just cause, and that being neither a robber nor a murderer, he did the same that many others were doing and that nothing capital could be pressed against him. But after his sentence his feelings were deeply acute. He became at intervals harsh and morose, and the great impression on his mind was that he had been unfairly put forward and confined, or sold, as he expressed it, to screen others who were more guilty than himself.' The author of this account comments on Dic's 'attention to religious exercises', but goes on, 'he often however complained that he had a stubborn and hard heart, and frequently said to those around him that if he had been a praying man and had avoided sabbath-breaking, drunkenness and immorality, he would not have been in that sad condition.' This, one suspects, rather than an admission of being involved in the riots, as suggested in the first report, is what he meant when he said that whatever his other failings, he was not guilty of the stabbing. He was, it seems, fond of a drink from time to time, and to someone with his solid Methodist background, what to us today are relatively trivial actions could appear to be major sins.

The actual execution is described briefly. Dic's 'surprising courage and firmness' are acknowledged, as are the sorrow of all concerned and their efforts on his behalf. But then one comes to what was perhaps the point of this narrative: Dic has already been shown to be a less than admirable character, but now his innocence is challenged.

> It is also satisfactory to the cause of the administration of the laws and of good order, that one of his fellow prisoners called the attention of Mr. Woods, the governor of the prison, and others, to a scar or wound on the outside of the right leg near the knee, which his fellow culprits saw him dress at Merthyr after his captivity, and understood to have been made by a bayonet. This the governor and several respectable persons connected with the prison, found as described, by which it would seem that the poor man, from a natural desire to save his life, and especially to screen his family from disgrace, which was a point very near to his heart, had erred when he said he was not near the affray, although it may be believed he was unconscious of having inflicted any severe injury on any particular person.

This second report was anonymous. The author would appear to be someone who knew what had occurred in the gaol, and certainly, though he has his own slant on what Dic said, the ministers' accounts agree with the substance of the conversations. Although he is concerned to show Dic as guilty of the stabbing, he does not seriously try to blacken his character – even acknowledging Dic's 'surprising courage and firmness' on the scaffold, and the 'unusual' deep sorrow of those conducting the execution. But then he comes to the point of his story – the wound on Dic's leg and its implications.

Since this wound was not brought up at the trial, the suggestion is that the disclosure, if it happened, was after the trial. If so, then the most likely 'fellow prisoner' with a desire to confirm Dic's guilt was Lewsyn, frantic to dissociate himself from his co-condemned. We know that he gave a sworn affidavit that he had not known Dic until both men were in Cardiff Gaol; this statement was actually made after he had been reprieved, but he may not have known that himself at the time. His words to the ministers after Dic was hanged suggest inside knowledge and perhaps some kind of deal – if he had had nothing to lose, he would have revealed Dic's innocence.

In the end we cannot know the truth, if any at all, of the story in the second report. The only named witness is Mr Woods, and he said nothing either for or against it. Perhaps it is also worth noting that the surgeon at the gaol had recorded Dic's denial of wounding the soldier and of carrying arms – you would think that if Dic had a wound or scar which could give the lie to this denial, that the surgeon would at the very least have mentioned it. Whoever actually wrote this report, it was evidently intended to justify the actions of the authorities in Wales and in Westminster, and the prison Governor may well have felt discretion was the most useful response.

What is, however, curious is the writer's conclusion that Dic was trying not just to save his life but to spare the feelings of his family and save them from disgrace when he said that he was not in the struggle outside the Castle Inn, and he 'may be believed [to have been] unconscious of having inflicted any severe injury on any particular person'. If this was the case, as Sockett had tried hard to prove, then Dic was not guilty, wherever he had been at the time, since the charge was that he had *deliberately* stabbed Donald Black.

A week later, on 27 August, the propagandists returned to the fray – in the shape of 'A Correspondent', whose communication was reported by *The Cambrian*, rather than given verbatim.[2] They provided a lengthy account, discrediting everyone on the side of the defence – Dic himself, the people of Merthyr, the members of the deputation to the Castle Inn, and John Thomas. Only Price, 'whose humanity is proverbial', was spared – and even he is criticised for using John Thomas to gather evidence on Dic's behalf.

A substantial part of 'A Correspondent''s narrative is devoted to the tribulations of James Abbott, 'a quiet and inoffensive tradesman', whom 'a very large mob' forced to escape from his own home through a back window, taking his wife and children with him. 'Not a customer dares enter his shop to be shaved since the Assizes, nor can he venture out of his house after dark.' As to the deputation at the Castle Inn, one of them is said to have announced as they went in, "Damn them, I wish my knife was three or four inches in their bellies." John Thomas is accused of having 'violently threatened' Abbott on more than one occasion, swearing to 'be up with him' (get even), and yet also said to have been 'among the most busy and active in accumulating evidence against [Dic and Lewsyn]. On one occasion he said, "If you have not evidence enough, my brother Tom saw the soldier stabbed, out of a window."'

As to Dic's 'wound', 'A Correspondent' elaborates the story with gusto. 'After the conflict, Richard Lewis was seen at a place called the Wern, where, while conversing with a farmer, <u>a bayonet fell out of his sleeve</u>.' On the next day Dic was on Aberdare Mountain, 'where he talked with several persons', including 'a very respectable freeholder' and a farm servant, to whom he apparently 'showed both his wounded knee and a hand tied up in a bloody handkerchief'. Many of the 'several persons' also saw the bayonet in his possession. Whether Aberdare Mountain was quite so heavily populated on that day we cannot know, but the testimony of family and friends is that Dic and his friend John Evans were on the mountain laying low in order to avoid both the rioters and the authorities. (Curiously, Isaac Evans's father, John's brother, had apparently also gone into hiding at a local farm, though Isaac does not say why he did this.)

'A Correspondent' was not to go unchallenged. The 10 September issue of *The Cambrian* included a letter from 'A Man of Glamorgan', someone who was apparently a friend of Joseph Tregelles Price.[3] The writer begins by stating that Dic's sad fate was awarded to him 'by an upright Judge and Jury of his Peers, acting upon evidence, clear and satisfactorily adduced before them in open court'. Thus if there was any miscarriage of justice, the blame would lie with those who could have provided counter-evidence and did not do so. However, new evidence had altered the public view of the matter: Mr Price's activities had been based on the facts he discovered, and not just on abstract ideas of justice or a dislike of the bloody nature of the penal code. 'A Man of Glamorgan' hoped that Joseph Tregelles Price would publish the evidence that he had uncovered – it should be remembered that the statements that Price had gathered were not at that point in the public record, so though Price's friends might have had a general idea of what he had found, they would not have known the details.

This vagueness is presumably why the 'Man of Glamorgan' accepts that Dic was 'beyond all question, <u>somewhere</u> in the fray near the Castle Inn'. Next he turns to 'A Correspondent''s account of the wound on Dic's knee and the bayonet in his possession, which he seems to accept as fact, though he says that this is still not evidence as to Dic's guilt. (This is a curious variation on Bosanquet's comment in a letter to Melbourne that Joseph Tregelles Price's evidence could be true and yet Dic could still have been guilty.)

Evidently 'A Man of Glamorgan' had serious doubts as to the correctness of Dic's sentence, but he was very careful not to go too far in his concern for justice. One suspects that some may have seen Joseph Tregelles Price as too much of an idealist in this case, and as an acquaintance, perhaps a friend, of his, the writer of this letter was anxious not to be seen in the same way. On the other hand, whoever he was, it is clear that he was someone of standing, and that doubt about Dic's guilt was not confined to the young miner's associates.

Whether 'A Subscriber', who was the next to join in the exchange in the following issue,[4] was the same person as 'A Correspondent' is unknown, their letter was once again a critical attack on those who had doubts about Dic's sentence. Among other points, 'A Subscriber' elaborated the story of Dic's wounded leg, stating that Donald Black had sworn 'that the person who stabbed him had a flesh wound at the knee. On examination of the body, a newly cicatrised wound was discovered in the knee.' 'A Man of Glamorgan' replied on 20 September,[5] accusing 'A Subscriber' of 'ingenuity of invention' and 'scarcity of information'. He defended his own position and also that of Mr Price, who had been accused of 'having failed to prove any one of the many things promised'. At the end, though, 'A Man of Glamorgan' said that both he and Mr Price would be abstaining from any further discussion 'in the present state of local excitement', though Joseph Tregelles Price would be willing to prove his point 'at a proper time and in a proper place'.

This seems to have been the end of the debate. There were no more letters or reports in *The Cambrian* and Joseph Tregelles Price took things no further. Dic lay quietly in his grave, where no one could tell whether he had a scar on his knee or a wounded hand. The authorities were no doubt very pleased that the matter had ended so peacefully. They must have realised that they were fortunate that insisting on carrying out the execution had not led to any further disturbances.

All of those involved in the sequence of reports and letters remained anonymous. 'A Man of Glamorgan' was presumably a representative of the upper classes: he was a friend of Joseph Tregelles Price, praised the uprightness of the judge and jury, and was 'resolved to uphold the sanctity of those laws which protect me and my fellow citizens of all classes, in the enjoyment of our property and privileges'. Despite this, he was prepared to accept that in this case the law could have been misapplied, which makes one realise just how far Joseph Tregelles Price's intervention changed the case. If he had not decided to visit the two condemned men, in all probability Dic would have gone to his grave and been forgotten, as those condemned in earlier disturbances had been. Whether his petition helped to save Lewsyn from the gallows – bearing in mind that Bosanquet was already working towards that – we cannot know, but it can hardly have injured his cause. For Dic, even if he could not save him, Price was able to establish his innocence of the crime of which he was accused, something which had been on Dic's mind in the days before his execution. It also established Dic as a hero for all those who hate injustice. And Price's own position, as an influential ironmaster, meant that what he had to say would be listened to, where Morgan Howells, trying to reach the King to plead for a reprieve, was likely to have been pushed aside.

The other correspondents provide no evidence as to who they were. While the narrative about the various wounds and bayonets may be more fiction than truth, the impression they give is that these two (or was it one – was 'A Correspondent' also 'A Subscriber'?) were close to the authorities and aware of things the general public would not know. The purpose of the second execution report and the letters was to justify the execution, and though the author(s) could have been public-spirited gentlemen, one has to suspect something a little more devious. Price's campaign and Melbourne's stubbornness had left the authorities with a major problem. The threats against James Abbott were more noisy than dangerous – long-term, he was not even driven out of Merthyr – but both the workers and the more philanthropic gentry had been given a reason to cause trouble. In the end no one did – and 'A Correspondent' makes it clear why this was: 'These daring disturbers of the peace are narrowly watched, so as to ascertain the ringleaders of whom, it is to be hoped, a severe example will be made.' 'A Man of Glamorgan' and Joseph Tregelles Price may also have been persuaded against any further action on the basis that it would do more harm than good.

Although there is no definite evidence, one gets the impression that once Merthyr had been subdued, its inhabitants were too wary of the consequences to do more than keep their heads down and hope for the best. It is said that some of the victims of the shooting outside the Castle Inn crept away or were carried off, then died and were buried in secret for fear of the authorities. Whether anyone from Merthyr other than those involved attended the trials or the execution is not recorded, but it was said that Dic's wife had to walk down to Cardiff to see her husband for the last time – there was no one to offer her a lift. And the old man who remembered Dic's funeral only speaks of people from the Vale joining the procession. Even 50 years later, both Isaac Evans and the man who claimed to have met the real 'murderer' in Pennsylvania were concerned not to say too much in case they caused problems for anyone.[6]

The last official comment on the affair came from Daniel Jones, the chaplain at Cardiff Gaol, reporting to the Glamorgan Quarter Sessions the following October, as follows:

> The Chaplain considers Richard Lewis whose life was forfeited to the Law had a correct sense of his Sinfulness and of the necessity of pardon through the merits and mediation of a Redeemer, but that he lived and died under a mistake and misapprehension concerning the Sinfulness of the acts of Rioting in which they had all partaken.[7]

Perhaps it is putting too great a stress on a brief statement, but it is interesting that Daniel Jones speaks of Sinfulness, something which as a clergyman he no doubt felt that all men, including himself, were guilty of, but after that, only of the general rioting, not of the specific crime for which Dic was executed. Did he too – who, after all, was one of those closest to Dic in the last four weeks of his life – also doubt the correctness of the sentence?

Dic's story lived on in oral tradition, and there were two or three occasions when those present at or involved in the events of 1831 recorded their memories of those days. There were, of course, two versions of the oral tradition. One was the romantic tale of folk memory: no grass would grow on Dic's grave; a white bird sat on or followed the coffin as it travelled to Aberafan; he was refused burial at every church until they came to Aberafan; as he died, there was a clap of thunder and a flash of lightning. It was a continuing tradition too: on the day that the news was received of the confession by the man who had really stabbed Donald Black, a cross supposedly grew up in grass on Dic's grave. A particularly gruesome tale appeared in the *Rhondda Leader* on 2 June 1906, to the effect that when Dic was being tried he had proclaimed his innocence and predicted that if he were sentenced to death and hanged, the child his wife was expecting would be born deaf and dumb and remain so all her life.[8] In fact the infant who was the subject of this tale was not Dic's daughter, but the child of Dic's widow and her second husband, Dic's friend John Evans. The little girl was indeed deaf and dumb, but grew up, married and had a large family, and her descendants still live in the Rhondda.

Gwyn A Williams, in his history of the Rising, tells how his grandmother paid to see Dic's ear as an exhibit at a fair in Merthyr,[9] and this is a curious example of how fact mutates into folklore. Dic, of course, did not lose his ear in the riot, but the man in America who confessed to having stabbed Donald Black did have an ear missing.

These tales – the ear apart – are common themes in folklore: dramatic, but owing more to imagination than fact. For instance, the weather at the time of the execution was grey and drizzly; there was thunder and lightning a little later in the morning, but not at the moment of the hanging. Grass rarely grows on a flat gravestone. In a slightly less fanciful vein, there is evidence that people wanted to be connected with Dic's story even a century after his death. The novelist Gwyn Thomas tells of how his father took him up a Rhondda hillside in the early twentieth century and told him that down there was where they brought Dic Penderyn's body on its way to Aberafan,[10] while a letter in the *Western Mail* in 1933 described how the writer's ancestor, coming from milking, met someone who had been with the funeral procession.[11]

The other tradition is something else. Whoever Dic's family may actually have been, in Aberafan people remembered him. This is not entirely surprising. In the early nineteenth century the population of Aberafan was about three hundred souls, most of them related, and Dic was clearly – even as a boy – someone to be remembered. Also, though the immediate family may have moved to Merthyr, at least one member of it – John, the lime burner – still ended up living locally at Pyle, and there may have been other Lewis connections in the town. It was not until almost a century later that this particular tradition began to get into print, but we get occasional glimpses of the way in which the story remained alive in local memory over the years, passed down through the generations. For instance, there is a newspaper report from September 1964 of the ninetieth birthday celebrations of Albert Thomas, descendant of one of the burgess families of the town.[12] He is described as 'the well-known local historian, who is always ready to talk about origins and remains of the past in this area', and 'recalls his grandmother, Lisa Morfa (Griffiths) of Corlannau, telling him of her joining the small pilgrimage which walked to Pyle in 1831, to meet the cortege bringing the body of Dick Penderyn to Aberavon cemetery for burial.' (The detail of the 'small' pilgrimage is interesting, because at that point, just before the town's population began to increase rapidly, there would not have been a large number to join those already in the procession.) In 1907 Lewis Davies of Cymmer was discussing the origin of Dic's nickname with a correspondent in the press, while Leslie Evans, doyen of Port Talbot's local historians, told me how, as a boy in the 1920s, he and his friends tried to 'improve' the worn inscription on Dic's grave.[13] Clive Jenkins, the white-collar union leader, recorded how, when he was at the Central School in the 1940s, 'another boy told me about Dic Penderyn ... "the day the real murderer confessed – in Australia – a cross grew up in grass on his grave. Come and look for it."' And when in 1956 Harri Webb was researching in Aberafan for his pamphlet on Dic, an elderly lady came out of her house in the now demolished St Mary's Place and told him that Dic had been buried at dead of night, and St Mary's Church was orientated to his grave.[14] Strictly speaking, neither of these facts was true; but if, as is possible, he was reburied in a place of greater distinction or closer to his family when the church was rebuilt in 1858, then one can see how the story came to exist – the rebuilding did involve the moving of some graves and exhumations tend to be at night. Dic's story was clearly still alive locally, even almost two centuries after his death. Alan Jones, deacon and Treasurer of Carmel Chapel in the late 1980s, once commented that his middle name was Richard, after his grandfather, who in turn had been named after Richard Lewis.[15]

The story did get into print from time to time over the next century, though mostly in the Welsh language. Firstly there were the accounts of two of the ministers, Edmund Evans and David Williams, who were with Dic on the morning of his execution. These were published in *Eurgrawn Wesleyaidd* (see Appendices), and provide some useful insight into Dic's attitude as well as the details of the event. Then there are the newspaper reports of the deathbed confession of the 'true murderer' of Donald Black, later identified as Ieuan Parker of Cwmavon – though whether this was Cwmavon in

Monmouthshire or the village in the Afan Valley is unknown, and the early accounts do not name the man.[16] These reports seem to have begun with a note in *Y Fellten* on 9 October 1874. The journal was publishing the Revd Evan Evans Nantyglo's account of his travels in America, and in these he describes meeting a work inspector – a 'respectable man' – who told him about a fellow worker he had met in Pennsylvania. This man had died some years before, but had confessed to killing the soldier Donald Black, then fleeing to America, leaving Dic to pay the penalty. By the time the story reached the *Western Mail* a few days later, it had become a deathbed confession to the Revd Evan Evans.

Next an anonymous correspondent in *Tarian y Gweithiwr* – 'Our man in America' – elaborated further on the tale, once again with a number of dubious details. In fact, not everyone was convinced by this new information, as we will see.

Two letters appeared in *Tarian y Gweithiwr* in response to this article: one elaborating the story of the confession; the other from Isaac Evans – whose uncle had been with Dic during the riots and later married his widow – providing some valuable details about Merthyr during the riots as well as information about Dic himself. Later there was a report in *Y Drysorfa* of an interview with the old man who had witnessed the execution and the funeral as a boy, published in 1919 (though written some years earlier). Then in 1933 in the *Western Mail* James Evans, Dic's great-nephew, described how he was taken to see his great-aunt Sarah, Dic's sister, who had heard the news of the confession and was in tears because her brother had been vindicated. And finally one has Lewis Davies's chapter in *Ystoriau Siluria* (1921). Davies was a teacher and his book was aimed at children. He sees Dic as guilty of murder, and is clearly presenting him as an example of wasted ability – a lesson for his pupils. He puts the worst possible slant on Dic's behaviour, and yet still cannot quite avoid showing him as a hero, if one who was seriously flawed. It is his account that first puts the local traditions of Dic's childhood and family into print. Although he taught at Cymmer in the Afan Valley, Lewis Davies originally came from Hirwaun, and as a local historian, had access to the traditional material of both Aberafan and Merthyr. He also published a number of novels aimed at older children, the first of which was *Lewsyn yr Heliwr* (1922), in which Dic makes a very brief appearance. Islwyn ap Nicholas wrote the first English-language account of Dic's life: *Dic Penderyn* (1945). He was the son of Welsh-language poet and radical T E Nicholas ('Niclas y Glais'), and had access to the Welsh-language tradition. He seems to have picked up on Lewis Davies's account of Dic's childhood, but also expanded it – and the details he added suggest that he drew from the same local sources as Davies.

At this point one has to wonder why the tradition existed. Although Joseph Tregelles Price had proved that Richard Lewis was clearly innocent of the charge on which he was convicted, the evidence he provided was not publicly available, and many people both at the time of the execution and later believed him to be guilty – as, for example, did the ministers who were with him in the last two days of his life. Nicholas Cooke, who recently analysed the trial for the Welsh Law Society, but apparently had no knowledge of the evidence found by Joseph Tregelles Price, also came to the conclusion that the man in the dock was guilty. Then again, other men had been executed for participating in riots in Merthyr only a few years before Dic and their names are not remembered. So one has to ask: who was Dic Penderyn, why was he killed, and why is he remembered? Was he merely 'a face in the crowd', as Gwyn Alf Williams suggested; taken at random to satisfy the need for a scapegoat, after being picked up because he had annoyed someone – or was there something else going on? Why was Lord Melbourne so determined that he would hang?

Perhaps one needs to look not just at events in Merthyr for an answer, but at a much wider picture. The events of 1831 took place only 12 years after the infamous Peterloo Massacre, when someone gave the wrong order and a detachment of cavalry rode down an innocent crowd gathered in St Peter's Fields, Manchester to listen to a speech on Parliamentary Reform given by the orator Henry Hunt. The government of the day had been heavily criticised for this incident. Merthyr was different: the crowd were armed with sticks and clubs and were pushing against the soldiers, disarming them, even invading the entrance to the Castle Inn. But at least 16 people were killed – some of them innocent bystanders, not even part of the crowd: one stray bullet had killed an old woman sitting knitting in her own living room. Admittedly this was in Wales, a distant and barbarous place, and the majority of the dead had been part of an unruly mob, not middle-class spectators in a great city, but Melbourne must have realised that criticism would follow and justification for the deaths would be needed. Hence, perhaps, the choice of Donald Black. No soldiers had died and others were perhaps more badly wounded, but Black's profusely bleeding thigh was more dramatic than a battered head and more easily claimed to be deliberate.

The authorities did not only have Peterloo to bear in mind. 1830 had been a year of popular revolutions: in France King Charles X had been overthrown, and though his successor was his cousin (Louis Philippe, Duke of Orleans), this was no longer a hereditary monarchy but now a matter of popular choice. The fact that Charles X had fled to Britain after being forced to abdicate brought these events very close to home. Belgium too had risen up against Dutch rule and declared independence. There were also risings in Italy, Poland and Switzerland, and though there were no obvious signs of revolution in Britain, the events in Merthyr just one year later must have caused major disquiet for the government. Those on the spot in Wales seem to have realised that the affair was not a prelude to revolution, hence the comparatively light sentences and the lack of any prosecutions concerning anything but the riots. No one wanted to advertise the fact that the workers in Merthyr had kept the army at bay for several days.

There was undoubtedly a third factor involved. The Merthyr Rising predates the growth of Trade Unions in the immediate area, but only just – they were already being created in the eastern valleys, and they were seen as a major threat by Melbourne and his fellows. Unions were a product of the Industrial Revolution, before which there had not been the kind of accumulation of workers that would make the idea of a union viable. The Guilds had regulated trade and conditions in earlier centuries, and there were social sanctions too – the kind of activity at grassroots that a little later led to the Rebecca Riots and in Merthyr lay behind the attack on the Court of Requests. The chapels, too, played a part. When William Abraham ('Mabon'), the future trade-union leader and MP, and his fellows returned early from their work in South America, they were summoned before the elders of Zion Chapel in Cwmafan to explain why they had apparently broken their contract. But the Guilds were basically employers' organisations, the chapels were moving into respectability, and the sanctions that worked in a village society could easily get out of hand in a looser context. And none of these put the ordinary working man first.

Unions were another matter. They involved bodies of workers who did put their own interests first – something that the ironmasters and their fellow industrialists can hardly have welcomed, because strength in numbers would give the men a voice. These early proto-unions often involved secrecy because some union activities could be seen as outside the law. It was the taking of a secret oath that was the 'crime' of the Tolpuddle Martyrs in 1834. We tend not to think of official surveillance as affecting our everyday lives, but of course it does, and any government would be remiss if it did not watch for possible dangers. The problem arises when their concern is not so much for national security as for their own status and authority. At a time like that of the Merthyr Rising, with agitation for Parliamentary Reform and unrest over domestic issues like falling wages and rising prices, not to mention the situation in Europe, the government must have been particularly sensitive to any threats, real or imagined. If they could get a possible troublemaker, one noted for standing up for workers' rights, out of the way, that would be a bonus. Judge Bosanquet, a man of the law, was willing to consider that the conviction might be unsound, though he never quite admitted that Dic was innocent. Melbourne, however, was adamant. He may not even have looked at Joseph Tregelles Price's second, much more detailed, petition – the one that finally swayed Bosanquet.

Some idea of the official response to this growth of workers' solidarity can be gathered from a report in *The Cambrian* on 10 September 1831, headed 'EXTREME CRUELTY':

On Monday the 5th inst., James Williams, formerly of Melin Griffith, began to work as a roller at Dowlais Iron Works, instead of a man who had been discharged. It seems that the poor fellow was not a member of the Union Clubs at that place, and during his work great numbers of the workmen assembled around, without actually molesting him; - he was however alarmed by what he saw, as he was heard to say, "I think I shall be killed tonight." Owing to the state of confusion he was in, or from some other unfortunate cause, he reached one of his legs too far back, and it was entangled in the level wheel, and so mangled as to require instant amputation high up the thigh. The poor fellow (considered as an interloper) was left a considerable time on the ground in the most wretched and agonized condition, before any of the numbers around him would render him the least assistance or even pick him up! Mr. Guest had him removed to one of his agent's houses, where every attention is paid to the poor sufferer. On the following day, another poor fellow belonging to the Plymouth Coal Works at Merthyr, was overwhelmed by a fall in the works, and one of his arms broken. The other colliers saw him under the fall, *and refused to assist him "because he was not of the Union."* The poor creature was left there to struggle out as well as he could. After extricating himself, he *fainted* on the road, where he was left by his fellow workers, unpitied and unaided! Surely no *"Union"* can be prosperous where "Brotherly love" appears so entirely absent.·

In fact it appears that these stories were at best exaggerations – the union men *had* come to the aid of the collier, and *The Cambrian* printed a retraction on 8 October – but the piece is of interest as an illustration of attitudes at the time. Whether they were official propaganda or just overblown rumour, stories like these were bound to lead to apprehension among the voting classes.

The account is followed by a piece on the Cumberland colliers who had apparently been dismissed because they wanted to form a 'combination'. They had now given this up and had been allowed to return to work. This, so *The Cambrian's* reporter stated:

...never would have been known here had it not been for the interference of incendiaries, calling themselves delegates, from an adjoining county, whose machinations have been completely foiled by a returning sense of duty among the very men they came to corrupt.

The true cause of their dismissal (for they never struck) was their avowed intention to form what they termed a "Union" with a view to the ulterior purpose of dictating (such, at least, has invariably been the practice wherever Unions have been established) what men should be retained at work or discharged, and other unlawful measures equally hostile to and destructive of all order and regularity. The melancholy consequences which have arisen from such dangerous combinations in various parts of the kingdom rendered such a project altogether inadmissible, and the works in the different pits were therefore suspended until the workmen should become sensible of the impropriety of their conduct, and evince their sincerity by relinquishing the proposed association. This object has been at length happily effected, and though several of the most violent characters amongst the colliers might have been fairly marked as ringleaders, and justly deprived of future employment; yet we have reason to believe that a very small number indeed, if any, are destined to experience the unpleasant effects of their reprehensible conduct.

This is clearly written from the employers' viewpoint, but it does give a useful picture of just how worried the authorities were about the rise of the unions. The details given of the fates of James Williams and his fellow worker seem to have been elaborated well beyond the actual events, but there are echoes in the second piece of the concerns of the Merthyr workmen – they too were concerned about losing their employment. And it has always been true that righteous anger about what are seen to be injustices can lead to consequences that no one either intended or wanted. It is interesting, too, to note the comment on 'incendiaries' corrupting the Cumbrian workmen; both sides, one suspects, had their *agents provocateurs*. Then there is the comment about the ringleaders being 'fairly marked' for punishment – which brings us back to the question: 'Why Dic?'

As has been suggested earlier, the sentences passed at the Assizes after the rioting in Merthyr were comparatively light. Though a number of death sentences were handed down, those sentenced were almost all recommended to mercy, but a scapegoat, or scapegoats, had to be found. Lewsyn yr Heliwr was an obvious choice: he had urged the crowd on outside the Castle Inn and was seen as a leader. Dic was another matter. He does not feature in any of the reports until his arrest, and as Joseph Tregelles Price undoubtedly proved, he was not in the melee outside the Castle Inn after the workers' deputation came out, yet the special constables made a point of going to his house to arrest him. Isaac Evans suggests that Dic had had an argument with Shoni Crydd and was on the special constables' blacklist, which was why he was on Aberdare Mountain, hiding out in case they targeted him.[17] Would they really, in those circumstances, with a crowd of rioters to round up, have gone after one man whose only crime had been to annoy one of their number? And, if it comes to that, would James Abbott really have sworn away a man's life on the basis of just a scuffle in a dark street a few weeks before? Or was Dic – a recognisable figure in Merthyr, a keen defender of workers' rights, fluent in both Welsh and English, knowledgeable – already a marked man? Isaac Evans says that his fight with Shoni Crydd caused not ill feeling, but suspicion, and the anonymous reporter who met the real 'murderer' in the United States also felt Dic had been deliberately set up. The old man who told the story of Dic's funeral said, 'The masters were afraid of him.'

There was, of course, one witness who was present in court and could, even in those circumstances, have said something to exonerate Dic: Lewsyn. Immediately after the execution he said that he knew who had actually stabbed Donald Black and if he too had been standing on the scaffold, he would have declared that Dic was innocent. Was that his bargain – that if he kept quiet, and ensured that Dic would be condemned, he could save his own life? In his address after the jury had given their verdict, Bosanquet had commented with regard to Lewsyn: 'Under all these circumstances, seeing the part that you have taken in the early part, and the leading part that you have taken throughout ... I cannot, however carefully I may have looked through this case, find any circumstances to justify me [in recommending you to the Royal Mercy]. I cannot, therefore, hold out to you any hope of a reduction of that sentence which it is my duty to pronounce.' Yet only three days later, though he had now moved on to the next set of Assizes, Bosanquet was already concerned about Lewsyn's sentence. His first letter to Lord Melbourne, on 17 July, does not suggest a reprieve and rather seems to be justifying his sentence. Then on 21 July he writes again to Melbourne to say that he has been told that Lewsyn saved the life of the special constable John Thomas, and he was therefore sending to Cardiff to respite the execution, and proposed following this in a few days with a reprieve. It would seem that someone had been talking to him, at first perhaps just to suggest the need to rethink Lewsyn's sentence, and then, when that did not seem to be having the desired effect, providing the information about Shoni Crydd which would allow Bosanquet to justify his change of heart.

If the authorities were merely looking for a scapegoat, both to cover any official embarrassment and to provide a serious warning of the consequences of rebellion, then Lewsyn would have made the perfect example. He had certainly been a leading figure, urging the mob to violence, bearing arms, attacking the soldiers. Obviously the authorities had realised this, which was no doubt why they put him on trial a second time, along with Dic, to point out that he was not just another one of the rioters. But in the end it was Dic who was intended to die, and if this meant letting Lewsyn survive, that was acceptable. He would, after all, be out of the way in Australia.

As for Dic himself, both *The Cambrian*'s accounts of the execution note that he felt himself to have been singled out, not just as a scapegoat, but to screen others more guilty than himself. The second account, with its dubious tale about the wound on Dic's leg, comments, with a curious echo of the words of Aaron Williams in 1800, that he had said he was dying for thousands. At least, in Dic's case, the thousands remembered him.

Postscript

Dic was gone, but others remained.

Lewsyn was duly transported to Australia alongside his fellow convicts and, though there were stories that he had returned home to south Wales, he eventually died in Australia shortly after his sentence had expired.

Dic's wife Elizabeth remarried a few years later. Her second husband was Dic's friend John Evans, and the couple's descendants still live in the Rhondda.

Dic's sister Elizabeth died aged only 41, leaving a young family. Morgan Howells married again and continued his career as one of the leading preachers of the day, but he too died while still comparatively young. He was not the 'hellfire, down with the workers' figure that many later writers assumed him to be – as mentioned earlier, via Hope Chapel in Newport he had links with John Frost and those involved in the Newport Chartist rebellion.

John and Matthew, Dic's brothers, both had families, and their descendants were among those who presented a petition for a pardon for Dic to Parliament in July 2016. Pamela Lewis, who often attended the Cardiff commemorations of Dic's execution, told me that these branches of the family had a proud tradition of trade-union activity.

Sarah, Dic's other sister, later married a John Morgan and lived in Newport, where the young James Evans – Morgan and Elizabeth's grandson – visited her after the news that a man in America had confessed to stabbing the soldier. Sarah was in tears to hear that her brother had been vindicated. Descendants have told me that the family were ashamed of what happened to Dic, not because they thought he was guilty, but because of the stigma of a family member being hanged as a criminal.

For many years there was a certain ambiguity about Dic's reputation. As noted earlier, many people – perhaps because they could not quite believe that someone could be executed simply for wounding – have assumed that Donald Black was killed. Also, Joseph Tregelles Price's evidence was not given in public, and it only seems to have been when Alexander Cordell unearthed the official records and included them as an appendix to his 1972 novel *The Fire People* that these became available. However, guilty or not, Dic was remembered as a martyr for the workers' cause, and in 1966 a memorial organised by local trade unionists was unveiled on his grave at St Mary's Church, Aberafan.[18] Earlier than this, when the National Eisteddfod came to Aberafan in 1932, hundreds of people visited the churchyard. Apparently there was then a headstone on the grave, and the inscription on this had been renovated 'thanks to the generosity of local friends'. (The inscription on the flat stone actually covering the grave, at least that section supposedly referring to Dic, has been more or less illegible for over a century.) The grave has now become so frequently visited that a path has been laid to it and a notice board giving details of Dic's story has been placed nearby. A commemoration is held there each year on the Sunday nearest to 14 August, the date of the funeral.

Initially Merthyr was perhaps still recovering from the major trauma that the aftermath of the rising had, very understandably, produced, and even an NUT history of Merthyr published in the 1930s scarcely noted the event. We know from Gwyn A Williams that the oral tradition had never forgotten the story, but in more recent years the town has also officially commemorated the events of 1831, and a plaque in memory of Dic has been placed on the Central Library. Merthyr is also home to the Dic Penderyn Society, whose Chairman, Viv Pugh, was part of the delegation that took the 2016 petition for a pardon to Westminster.

Cardiff for several years had its own commemoration, organised by the late Charlie Gale, trade unionist and city councillor, and held on the site of the old Cardiff Gaol – now the Market, where there is a plaque at the St Mary Street entrance. Each of these events has, or had, its own particular emphasis. In Aberafan, it has been Dic himself; in Merthyr, where the commemoration is held in May, it has been the Rising and the story of workers' rights; in Cardiff it was associated with the wider story of social justice. When Charlie Gale died, Rhodri Morgan, the First Minister of the Welsh Assembly, took on the organisation of the event, but after he was taken ill, no one else has yet taken up the baton.

In an article for *Llafur* in September 1978, Gwyn A Williams suggested that perhaps all this celebration was wrong because it commemorated someone who was a victim, not an activist like Lewsyn and his fellow workers. In practice it is often Lewsyn who dominates the story because we know more about him – and Lewsyn does deserve his place as one of the heroes of June 1831. He was one of those whom circumstances elect as a folk hero, someone to whom his fellows listened, and without him events might have got very much worse. He saved the life of Shoni Crydd, quite possibly at the risk of his own, and he insisted on a degree of order and justice in what went on before the tragedy outside the Castle Inn. Admittedly his incitement of the crowd was a contribution to the violence that happened after the deputation came out of the inn, but by then events were well beyond anyone's control.

As to Dic, for Gwyn A Williams he was simply a victim, not worthy of being remembered. Yet there are two kinds of victims. There are those who are sacrificial lambs, who are simply in the wrong place at the wrong time, and there are those who die because of who they are and what they have done, who do not accept victimhood. They may not have won the battle, but their cause is not lost. Richard Lewis refused to be a victim: he died with a challenge on his lips, not a whimper, and his words still echo – an assertion of right and an acceptance of responsibility.

20 years after Dic's death the workers of his birthplace defied the Bank of England and its officials over a matter of religious intolerance and won. Some of those men and women may well have been among the crowd in St Mary's Street on 13 August 1831. They too fought injustice.

CHAPTER 7

Afterlife

WALES IS STILL waiting for its Sir Walter Scott to bring its history to colourful life, but there *are* a few characters who have attracted their chroniclers. Owen Tudor, secret husband of Queen Catherine de Valois and grandfather of Henry VII, features in several romantic novels, as does Princess Nesta, the so-called 'Helen of Wales'. Owain Glyndwr has also found his interpreters. Edith Pargeter, better known perhaps as Ellis Peters, the author of the Brother Cadfael stories, has produced a fine quartet of novels about Llywelyn ap Gruffudd ('Llywelyn the Last') and his brothers, as well as a trilogy set in the early medieval Welsh Border country. Later centuries have been less popular and conditions rather than characters have provided the central focus for historical fiction based in Wales in those years. Dic Penderyn/Richard Lewis is an exception, appearing in at least four novels, in three of which he is a leading character.

However, his first entrance into popular culture was in verse, not prose, and came soon after his death. Dic Dywyll, the blind ballad singer, published 'a new song giving the history of the execution of Richard Lewis (Dic Penderyn), which took place on the 13th of August 1831, in Cardiff, Glamorganshire, for the crimes of which he was guilty during the late disturbances in Merthyr Tydfil'.[1] The ballad is some 22 quatrains in length but Dic does not appear until verse 15 – the earlier section deals with the disturbances and the terrible consequences of the confrontation outside the Castle Inn. Although verse 17 explains that 'Squire Price' managed to get a fortnight's delay from the original date of the execution, it gives no details of his campaign, and Dic's guilt seems to be taken for granted. The role of the prison chaplain in advising the condemned man to recognise Jesus Christ as his saviour is noted, and the ballad makes a point of Dic's final prayer to Jesus, to take him into Heaven. It ends with what is effectively a pious wish that God will preserve Britain and keep everyone from offending against the law of the land; God's laws are in our hearts, but our lives are in the hands of men.

Precise details of Dic Dywyll (a.k.a. Richard Williams)'s career are unknown. He was probably born in Anglesey, perhaps near Llannerch-y-medd, but as a ballad singer he travelled all over Wales and is chiefly associated with Merthyr Tydfil. His name does not appear in the accounts of the disturbances, but local tradition suggests that he was the blind man who was one of the speakers at the meeting at Twyn y Waun that led into the riots. He wrote another ballad about the events of those first days in June 1831, with the suggestion that the crowd went too far – his comment that they were 'against the good/just laws of the kingdom' is an odd echo of the comments of 'A Man of Glamorgan' in *The Cambrian* after the execution. His ballad about Dic Penderyn was very popular, and it is instructive to look at what he says – or does not say – about his subject. The title of the ballad, which declares that Dic Penderyn died for the crimes he had committed, may, of course, be the printer's comment, not that of the author of the ballad. Dic Dywyll himself notes only his subject's piety at the last. He does not mention that final furious cry of defiance.

This was not Dic's only appearance in verse. A rather more literary version is John Stuart Williams's *Dic Penderyn: A play for voices*, commissioned by BBC Wales and broadcast in 1968. The text was included in Williams's 1970 collection,

Dic Penderyn and other Poems. Williams tells what might be called the standard version of the story, stressing the injustice suffered by the workers of Merthyr as compared to the ironmasters, who are 'cold and hard as the metal you make'. The only mention of the Court of Requests is in passing, without explanation: 'Your ramshackle court is burned to the ground.' Dic and Lewsyn are friends, drinking together in a tavern, and Abbott and Shoni Crydd watch for a chance to injure Dic. There is no definite mention of Dic as one of the delegation, only 'Were you at the Castle Inn?' 'Ask those who were there', and he is confused with Lewsyn – captured in the woods above Abernant, not taken from his bed late at night. In a way, one might say that he is absent from his own story, characterised only as an 'easy spirit who finds it hard to hate'. The limitation of time – only 30 minutes allowed for the programme – meant that it was never going to be an in-depth study of either the riots or Dic, but Lewsyn, as he has a tendency to do elsewhere, takes the narrative over.

The play itself is a stirring mixture of free verse narrative and dialogue, with four short ballads inserted at intervals. It is one of a series of similar verse-plays commissioned by BBC Wales over a decade or more, whose writers often chose historical themes. The writers were limited to a cast of four actors, but that gave a fair degree of flexibility for storytelling, and in this case a folk singer was included to open and close the drama.

There may have been other ballads over the years, but it seems to have been the unveiling of the monument on Dic's grave in 1966 that marked the start of a more recent flow of poems, songs and even a musical about the Merthyr Rising and its martyr. Welsh-language folk-music icon Meic Stevens wrote the song 'Dic Penderyn' in 1972 after reading Gwyn Thomas's *All Things Betray Thee* (see below); singer-songwriter Martyn Joseph was inspired to write a track on the same theme for his 1996 album *Full Colour Black & White*; Huw

Pudner and Chris Hastings, stalwarts of the annual Penderyn commemoration at St Mary's, Aberafan, contributed a folk song, *The Gates of Cardiff Gaol*; and the folk-rock group The Chartists set a poem by John Stuart Williams to music in 1987. Alun Rees, an affiliate of the Red Poets of Merthyr, was another who provided a poem on the subject. Then the spring of 2017 saw the arrival of *My Land's Shore*, a musical about the Merthyr Riots by Christopher J Orton and Robert Gould. Its official world premiere was in Ye Olde Rose and Crown Theatre in Walthamstow in London in 2017, to considerable acclaim, and it was performed at Theatr Soar in Merthyr Tydfil in February 2018.[2] However, it had made its very first appearance in a concert performance at The Gate, Cardiff in 2007, directed by Craig Revel Horwood of *Strictly Come Dancing* fame, who said, 'I was drawn in by its powerful story and beautiful, soaring score … a Welsh *Les Mis*.'

As it happened, *My Land's Shore* was not the first musical, and it is interesting to see how far the story had travelled from Merthyr. In 1980 two teachers at the Cheney School in Oxford, Chris Wright (History) and Chris Banks (Music), created a musical play for their 13–16-year-old pupils. The 13 songs and choruses included *The Iron Men of Merthyr*, *Up the Waun to See the Fair*, *Playing with Fire* and *Goodbye to All the Years*.

Folk songs and musicals were not the only dramatic presentations of the Merthyr story. In 1996 Gwyn Thomas's novel *All Things Betray Thee* was dramatised by Alan Plater and broadcast by the BBC. Much earlier than that, there had been the first night of *Jackie the Jumper*, Gwyn Thomas's own play. Jackie Rees, the 'Jumper' of the title, who might be described as an amalgam of Dic, Lewsyn and Thomas Llewellyn, was played by Ronald Lewis, who was himself from Aberafan.[3] *Jackie the Jumper* was Gwyn Thomas's second play; his first, *The Keep*, a naturalistic drama set in a contemporary Valleys family home, had had its premiere at the Royal Court Theatre in 1961, to some acclaim. *Jackie the Jumper* followed this, also at the Royal Court, opening on 1 February 1963, and must have provided something of a shock if the audience had been expecting something similar. The text of the play was published in full in the February edition of *Plays and Players* magazine, with an introduction by the author. After describing his theatrical background and enjoyment of melodrama, Thomas ends with a note on the setting and characters of the play:

> For the story of *Jackie the Jumper*, the facts are loosely set in the context of the early Chartist movement, the Merthyr Riots to be exact. Involved in them is Jackie the Jumper, and facing him is his uncle, Richie 'Resurrection' Rees, a thundering divine. And between them the early struggles of a society tormented and besmirched by the eruption of the great iron furnaces and the descent of the great puritanical vetoes.

The first act of the play is set in the open air, with the glare of the furnaces in the background, and introduces Jackie himself. He is a figure from the world of myth and legend, a free spirit, a trickster, a 'shatterer of fresh maidens and subverter of honest artisans', a wanderer through the world. He is also a leader. Opposed to him is his uncle, the Reverend Richie Rees, a hellfire and brimstone preacher, determined to destroy all that his nephew stands for, even if it means Jackie's death. Just to annoy him, Jackie encourages his friends to enjoy a small orgy. Act Two is set in the dining room of John Luxton, the ironmaster. He has been entertaining the County Sheriff, the Colonel of the County Militia and the Revd Richie Rees, and Luxton's three daughters are also present. Luxton, the play's version of William Crawshay, talks of his unhappiness at being expected to act the tyrant – he had once wanted to be a painter and has some sympathy for his workmen. Slowly the sounds of rebellion grow in the background, and finally Jackie is brought in, a prisoner threatened with execution. But his followers break in and free him, taking Luxton, his guests and his daughters prisoner instead. Act Three is set in the bar of the

Rising Lark inn, on the top of a hill. Luxton and the others are here, held hostage, but the soldiers have surrounded the hill and there is, seemingly, no escape for Jackie. Richie Rees, the Sheriff and the Colonel each in their own way bribe Jackie's followers into deserting their leader, and finally the soldiers come for him. But he is, after all, the trickster. 'Run hard, Jumper,' Luxton tells him, and he walks out into the twilight, Luxton's coat over his shoulder.

Jackie is clearly not the historical Dic Penderyn, who was never accused of shattering maidens, nor is he Lewsyn, though he borrows something of Lewsyn's power of leadership. Luxton has something of the ambiguity of the William Crawshay of history, but Richie Rees is no copy of the real Morgan Howells, though tradition has tended to see him as Dic's antagonist. However, in the 1950s and early 1960s Gwyn Thomas would have had no access to any serious studies of the Merthyr Rising and so his play is an echo of popular tradition. At one point Aaron Mead, a blind, prophetic ironworker, says:

> Ever since my eyes went in that furnace blast, I have had a vision. The vision of one of our own kind, killed for us. A gay, laughing one, to whom life means more than for the rest of us. Somebody in whom the dousing of light would have darkened the whole earth ... They would have hanged him in the County town. We would have asked for his body for burial in his home town ... We'd have put his body on a farm-cart to strike the note of humility. We'd have followed it to its grave, over the ridges, through the fields, and on the way we'd have sung and wept ... A tremendous funeral ... And [his] spirit would have gone to provide one more flame for the dawn of a beckoning restitution.

Interestingly, in what is an exuberantly wordy play, full of Thomas's typical baroque use of language, this brief speech – the only one directly applicable to the story of Richard Lewis – is a simple echo of the actual event. Gwyn Thomas the grown man never forgot the day when his father took him as a young boy up the mountain above the Rhondda, pointed down the valley and told him, 'This is where they brought the coffin of Dic Penderyn on its way to Aberavon.'

In addition to these stage and radio plays, Dic has made his appearance in several television programmes. Gwyn Alf Williams, a Merthyr boy himself and author of *The Merthyr Rising*, was involved in a number of TV presentations, but for him Dic was merely a face in the crowd – even something of a simpleton – picked out at random to provide the necessary scapegoat. This was finally spelt out in full in a half-hour programme, one of the historian's last projects. It appears that Williams had been told, years earlier, that Dic was more or less the local village idiot, something he hesitated to indicate until that last programme, but which probably contributed to Dic's low profile in *The Merthyr Rising*.[4]

For just over a century the story of Dic Penderyn was recorded mostly in the Welsh language and in articles in periodicals or the occasional newspaper reference. Even the centenary of his execution produced only a few letters in the *Western Mail*, and even then not in the actual year of the centenary. There was, however, one piece which was rather more than a reminiscence: a chapter in Lewis Davies's *Ystoriau Siluria*. Davies came originally from Hirwaun, but was a schoolmaster in Cymmer in the Upper Afan Valley from 1886 onwards. He wrote mainly for children and *Ystoriau Siluria* (1921) is a collection of tales about historical characters like Llywelyn the Last or the pirate Colyn Dolphyn, as well as more local figures like Canaythen of Margam (taken hostage and blinded by the Norman Earl of Gloucester) or the Red Vicar of Glyncorrwg. The stories were clearly meant to provide moral lessons for their young readers. Though not an antiquarian like his neighbour Cadrawd at Llangynwyd, whose collections helped to form the Welsh Folk Museum at St Fagans, Davies had published a short history of the Afan District, and had

131

written to the press about Dic several years earlier. To him Dic was *rhyfygus* (rash or foolhardy: 'out of control' as we might say today), and the incident when Dafi Cound fell into the harbour was Dic's fault for losing his temper, and the reason he went off to Merthyr. As to the events in that town, Davies sees Dic as a leader in all the turmoil, a loyal second to Lewsyn, and in his version Donald Black was killed, not wounded, in the fighting and Dic was responsible.

This is a curious mixture of fact and fiction. Davies states that the soldier was killed, but stresses that Dic always denied having harmed him. Later he describes the funeral procession to Aberafan but says there was no service, only the singing of a Welsh hymn – given out by Dic's old schoolmaster, in his version one David Jones. Perhaps the importance of the story is not so much the correctness of its details, but rather the evidence it provides that there was a strong local tradition about Dic's early life and also that he was still widely remembered almost a hundred years after his death. As we have seen, the disturbances in Merthyr were not unique, even in the town itself, and the Chartist Rising at Newport and the Rebecca Riots were major events that might well have been expected to have eclipsed the earlier one. Perhaps the sad tale of an innocent man, condemned to death by a heartless judiciary, might have lingered – but as we have seen, not everyone believed in Dic's innocence, then or now. Although he spent most of his life in Cymmer, Davies was originally a native of Hirwaun and perhaps his image of Dic owes something to that. Those who signed Taliesin ap Iolo's petition did, after all, assume that Dic and Lewsyn were guilty.

D Emrys Lewis was the next to cover the story. His first article was published in the *Welsh Outlook* in 1931, followed by a second in the *Transactions of the Aberafan and Margam Historical Society* three or four years later. Lewis added some interesting details – for instance that Dic had composed a hymn in his last days in gaol, and that his handcuffs had been kept by the family of the High Sheriff of that time, Richard Hoare Jenkins. Jenkins had been in attendance at the execution and called it the most difficult of his civic duties.[5] However, it was the 1940s that saw the first fuller texts: Islwyn ap Nicholas's short biography (1945) and two novels: Michael Gareth Llewelyn's *Angharad's Isle* (1944) and Gwyn Thomas's *All Things Betray Thee* (1949). Exactly why this was the case is not clear. A history of Merthyr Tydfil published by the local NUT *c.*1930 hardly mentions the riots, let alone Lewsyn or Dic, and the detailed accounts of historians like David Jones and Gwyn Alf Williams still lay in the future. However, if anything, this makes these first two novels particularly relevant because they reflect the popular tradition regarding the events at Methyr and the characters involved.

Frederic Evans, who wrote under the pen name of Michael Gareth Llewelyn, was the son of Cadrawd, the local historian, antiquarian and blacksmith of Llangynwyd in the Llynfi Valley. Originally he and his father had planned to produce a history of the area, but it seems that the First World War intervened. Evans fought in the war and later became an Inspector of Schools, not returning to authorship until the 1940s, when he published children's stories, an autobiography and four novels.[6] *Angharad's Isle*, his first novel, is set in south Wales in the first decades of the nineteenth century and tells the story of the industrialisation of the region. Ynys Angharad, the 'Isle' of the title, is a farm in the Llangynwyd area, its fertile acres a symbol of the old, rich folk tradition, gradually eroded and marred by the stain of industry. The narrator is Dafydd Niclas, a harpist and singer and grandson of the Dafydd Niclas who was household bard and tutor to the Williams family of Aberpergwm in the Vale of Neath.

At Ynys Angharad, Dafydd comes across Phil the Collier. Phil has had some schooling, can read and is bilingual. He has read Thomas Paine's works and is a radical. He works on the farm, but also, from time to time, in one of the small local pits, hence his nickname. When the army recruiters come by, looking to press men into service, he hides from them, unwilling to be forced to serve – but later he volunteers and fights at Waterloo. This only strengthens his radicalism: 'When back I am, speak I shall for the soldier as well as the worker.'

A few years later, Dafydd and his father – who both share Phil's radical views – go to a great gathering in Penydarren where they are told that one Dic Penderyn, a 'fiery champion of the people's rights' will be speaking. This turns out to be Phil the Collier – now 'Dic' because his full name is Philip Richard Powel, and 'Penderyn' because that is where he is now living. Dafydd and Dic join forces, speaking to the workers of the need for unity, at first 'in the big rooms of some of the new public houses. But not long were the masters before realizing that against them and the truck system were these meetings. So on the mountainside we had to hold them instead.'

Slowly things develop until the confrontation outside the Castle Inn. Lewsyn is there, urging the crowd on, but in Llewelyn's story Dic is a leader in the business of the Court of Requests and the march on Penydarren and Dowlais. He is also involved in the defence of Merthyr against the soldiers, but in the end Dic and Lewsyn are captured and put on trial. Both are condemned to death, but Lewsyn is reprieved and Llewelyn queries the reason for this – was Lewsyn the son of a local coal owner, or a spy for the authorities? He offers no definite answer to this, but goes on to describe Dic's funeral. Dic is buried 'high upon the Eagle Mountain', attended by 'thousands of enraged, tearstained colliers and ironworkers'.

Llewelyn has clearly taken some liberties with his portrait of Dic. Phil the Collier fights at Waterloo in 1815 when Dic would have been 7, and is shown as a leader in the riots, in the roles actually held by Lewsyn and Thomas Llewellyn. These points, together with Dic's burial on the mythic Eagle Mountain, were evidently for dramatic effect – it is not credible that Llewelyn did not know of the burial at Aberafan. As the novel was published in London and aimed at an audience which was unlikely to be familiar with the details of the Merthyr Rising, it would certainly be more effective to make Dic the leader and have him buried on a wild mountainside.

However, Llewelyn was a local historian, aware of traditional lore as well as the documented version, and his portrait of Dic does offer a solution to a major problem. All the evidence suggests that Richard Lewis was deliberately picked as the necessary scapegoat, but the question remains, why? And why were Dic and the two Evans brothers sufficiently concerned that they might be set up as to go to ground after the events at the Castle Inn? There are suggestions that Abbott later admitted that he had lied in court – and there is evidence that his original statement was altered. Then there is the matter of Lewsyn's reprieve and his comment that he could (would?) have cleared Dic had he himself not been spared. Was his silence the price of his escape from the gallows?

As previously mentioned, we do not know if Dic could write. There are references to him writing letters and even a hymn in his last days, though it is possible that these could have been dictated. If he *was* able to write, then he could have been responsible for some of the radical pamphlets circulating at the time, and if the authorities had identified him as being behind them and seen him as a long-term threat, they would have had reason to dispose of him, given the opportunity. However, Llewelyn's Dic is an orator, travelling round, spreading the gospel of opposition to the tyranny of the ironmasters and the oppression of the poor in general. We know that such meetings were being held in the area around this time – if Dic and the Evans brothers involved and had come to the notice of the security services, that might explain them wanting to keep a low profile while the Rising was under way. And it could explain why Dic was remembered so widely, not just in Merthyr, and why the tradition was so lasting and so strong. It was not likely only to have been because he was considered innocent; Taliesin ap Iolo's petition apparently accepted that Lewsyn and Dic were guilty as charged, and though no doubt some people in Merthyr did believe him innocent and may have been aware that Joseph Tregelles Price was collecting evidence to prove it, the material he collected was not available to the public for well over a century. Lewis Davies certainly sees Dic as guilty of killing the soldier, as did Nicholas Cooke, working purely on the trial record.

In Gwyn A Williams's account, Dic was an innocuous bystander and Lewsyn the leader of the Rising, which makes it all the stranger that Dic was hanged and Lewsyn was reprieved – though transportation would, of course, ensure that the latter was permanently out of the way. But perhaps someone who, almost by accident, came to prominence in those days was less of a danger than a man who was knowledgeable, charismatic, a keen defender of workers' rights; who as an ironstone miner and haulier was part of the aristocracy of the workers and could preach his message every bit as eloquently as his brother-in-law. It might also explain why those discussing the story, from 'A Man of Glamorgan' in *The Cambrian* in 1831 to Isaac Evans and the anonymous correspondent in America decades later, suggested that it would not be wise to say too much about the case.

We have already discussed Gwyn Thomas as the author of the play *Jackie the Jumper*, but over a decade earlier he had published a novel, *All Things Betray Thee*, which also used the story of the Merthyr Rising. We know from Thomas's *A Few Selected Exits* that he had been introduced to Dic's legend when his father took the young boy up the mountainside, pointed down the valley and told him that that was where they had brought the coffin on the way to Aberafan. What else he was told, if anything, is not known, but it clearly made a serious impression on him and in 1949 he used the story as the basis for a novel. Technically it is a historical novel, but it hardly fits the standard format. It is written in Thomas's highly idiosyncratic style, though it lacks much of his usual black humour.

The novel is curiously detached from any precise date or setting – Wales is never mentioned and the places and people's names rarely seem Cymric. Merthyr is Moonlea, Tudbury seems to be a composite of Cardiff and Brecon, the hills around are Arthur's Crown and the Southern Mountains. Whether this is because Thomas wanted to universalise his theme or whether the well-attested reluctance of London-based publishers to accept texts set in Wales played a part remains unknown. The historical element too is a composite of the Merthyr Rising and the Chartist march on Newport, with a mention of the Rebecca Riots thrown in at one point, but all without any precise detail.

However, the major historical research and writing of men like David Jones and Gwyn Alf Williams did not begin to appear until the 1970s. Islwyn ap Nicholas's short biography of Dic Penderyn was published in 1945 but was based more on tradition than research. Thus Thomas's portrait of his hero, like that in *Angharad's Isle*, is likely to reflect the man more as he was remembered by the community than as he appeared from official records.

All Things Betray Thee is narrated by Alan Hugh Leigh, a harpist from 'the mountains of the North'. He has come south to look for his friend, John Simon Adams – they grew up together, but then John Simon came south to care for his father. Now Alan has inherited a small piece of land and has come to take his friend back to an idyllic life in the mountains. Alan is the eternal onlooker, watching but never getting involved, and he is not happy to find that John Simon *has* become involved and is unwilling just to up sticks and leave. Moonlea is dominated by the owners of the ironworks, especially Mr Penbury (who is very loosely based on William Crawshay) and by Lord Plimmon, the local landowner. Penbury is a closet radical, but his manager, Radcliffe, and Plimmon are tyrants, prepared to have those workers they see as dangerous murdered by a hired thug. There is a recession in the iron trade and Penbury is threatening to shut down the furnaces. The men are organising against them and John Simon plans a major, unarmed demonstration, but the Yeomanry have been sent for and a massacre ensues. John Simon and Alan are arrested, on a charge of having murdered Plimmon's hired assassin. They are tried, found guilty and sentenced to hang. Penbury, however, has taken a liking to the harpist and arranges for him to be pardoned. Alan, drawn in at last, helps to organise a rescue for his friend, but they are too late; John Simon has already been hanged.

Although Thomas does not show John Simon actually addressing public meetings as Llewelyn does, it is quite clear that he is an organiser, travelling round and meeting fellow workers across south Wales. He is already a marked man, someone the ironmasters want to remove from the scene. If one turns to the historical Dic Penderyn, this is not something that shows up in the official record, but there are hints at something similar. As a teenager, so it is said, he spoke out for the rights of his fellow workers and possibly lost his job as a result; later he was chosen as one of the deputation of 12 to meet the ironmasters (which Lewsyn was not); even many years later those who wrote about his story were wary of saying too much. If the authorities had merely needed a scapegoat for the killings outside the Castle Inn, then Lewsyn would have been an ideal candidate: a leader on that day, in the riots leading up to it and in the Rising afterwards.

If Michael Gareth Llewelyn and Gwyn Thomas were both drawing on an existing but unwritten tradition, then it would help to explain why Dic's life and death made such a strong impression, not just in Merthyr but across south Wales – his guilt or innocence may have been irrelevant here if what people were honouring was a champion of their own. Did the more respectable people of Cardiff stay away from the execution because they feared trouble or because they did not wish to countenance political murder? And why were the people of the Vale so concerned about the funeral of some unknown felon from Merthyr that they escorted his body to Aberafan? We will probably never know for certain who Dic was or what he might have accomplished, but he earned his place in history by more than simply being in the wrong place at the wrong time. There is a curious echo in the account of the funeral procession of another such occasion, when in 1821 vast crowds followed the body of the unpopular George IV's discarded Queen Caroline – who had come to be seen as a figurehead of the movement demanding reform – on its journey from London to Harwich, en route for Brunswick. The people could not prevent injustice but they *could* make their own verdict known.

The 1960s saw the rise of a new generation of Welsh historians. Llafur, the society for the study of Welsh Labour History, was established in 1970, but this was the formalisation of a movement that had already begun to publish its work. Hence, when Alexander Cordell began to write his novel *The Fire People*, a novel which drew on the story of the Merthyr Rising, he could use official sources and guidance to an extent that his two forerunners could not have done. In fact he went further and uncovered the texts of a number of the letters and petitions and part of the trial record, publishing them at the end of his novel. On the other hand, he probably did not have access to the long-standing local traditions that Llewelyn and Thomas knew, except perhaps through their novels.

The Fire People begins in Taibach with Gideon Davies, a half-blind fiddler who is playing for a wake. Soon he sets off for Merthyr and on the way picks up a companion called Sun Heron, who is thought to be Irish (though it is never quite clear whether Sun, who later becomes Dic's wife, is actually Irish or is Welsh). Although there are two brief references to 'a Welsh boy', it is not until page 100 that Dic Penderyn arrives, rescuing Gideon and Sun from the Cefn Riders, a gang of hooligans who in real life carried on their villainy near Pyle, but here are somewhere near Merthyr. It is soon clear that Dic is, if not a leader or an organiser, a keen supporter of the need for a union. Lewsyn appears almost halfway through the book, at an Oddfellows lodge/union meeting, where the matter of the Court of Requests is raised. Meanwhile Morgan Howells seems to be almost permanently staying with Dic's family, preaching hellfire sermons.

Finally the narrative reaches the meeting at the Waun and the events that followed. Dic is present during the riots, but not at the gathering outside the Castle Inn because Morgan Howells has persuaded him to go off with a 'Mr Evans', away from trouble – though one of the rioters thinks he has seen him there. The rising fails and Dic is arrested, tried and hanged, despite all the efforts to save him.

The Fire People is an odd mixture of bawdy baroque with earnest social concern. The sections covering Dic's story are relatively straightforward, but elsewhere the narrative is full of colourful characters with names like Billa Jam Tart and Dai End-On, or the Dylanesque Miss Blossom Thomas. Lemuel Samuel is borrowed, consciously or not, from *All Things Betray Thee*, though this time he is the manager of the Company Shop in Taibach and rather less villainous – like several of the other Taibach characters, he later turns up in Merthyr.

At the point when Cordell began to work on *The Fire People*, he was involved in a promotional tour for his previous book, *Song of the Earth*, which was set in the Vale of Neath, and so he started his preparatory research in the Port Talbot district. He intended to make the experiences of the Irish immigrants who were fleeing the Potato Famine *c*.1850 the theme of his book. However, he realised after a while that there had not been enough dramatic confrontations to make his story effective, so he turned to a second local theme, the story of Dic Penderyn. He had already written some 70 pages which he was loath to discard, and so, apart from the two passing references, Dic arrives on page 100. The Irish element did not disappear completely; apart from a number of characters of Irish origin, there are several dramatic passages describing the influx of those fleeing the Blight:

> The Irish immigrants were pouring in from Kenfig Sands: in their hundreds they came, the men scarecrowed with hunger, the tattered women with their skeleton babies lurching on their backs ... What began as a trickle grew into a flood of humanity that choked the Welsh lanes: they ate their way from barren Connemara, giving birth in the frozen fields, finding graves in wayside ditches.

Unfortunately, the Merthyr Rising took place almost 20 years before the tragedy of the Irish Famine, which leads to a number of anachronisms, but Cordell did take some trouble in researching Dic's story.

Cordell's Dic is brave – he helps to defeat the Cefn Riders and save Gideon and Sun Heron – and deeply involved in the campaign to set up a union, alongside Gideon and the foreign organiser Zimmerman. Although initially Dic is part of the mob repossessing the objects taken by the officers of the Court of Requests, Morgan Howells then more or less blackmails him into going with a 'Mr Evans' to keep out of the way of trouble and preserve his family's reputation. There is, though, a suggestion that Dic sneaks back for a while and *is* in the deputation – which, of course he was: in real life, he and John Evans only went to ground after the events at the Castle Inn. Generally speaking, Dic is shown as a good committee man rather than a leader, but even then he is a long way from the 'innocuousness' that Gwyn Alf Williams believes made him a martyr.

The Fire People picked up on an increasing interest in Dic and his story rather than causing it, but it certainly helped to promote that interest. Cordell's novel was not the last to take the story of the Merthyr Rising as a theme; 1975 saw the publication of *The Angry Vineyard* by Rhydwen Williams. Williams was best-known for his Welsh-language output, which included novels, plays and poetry, and twice won the Crown at the National Eisteddfod. He came originally from the Rhondda but at the time of writing this novel was living in Aberdare.

In researching *The Angry Vineyard*, Williams had access both to Welsh-language sources which were not available to at least two of the earlier novelists, and also to the new documents found by Cordell. He made use of all of this material to build up his picture of Merthyr and of Dic himself. The story he tells is relatively straightforward, beginning just before the unrest starts to grow and ending with Dic's funeral. Dic and Lewsyn are good friends, while James Abbott is Crawshay's lackey and spy. Morgan Howells is frequently there, trying to persuade Dic not to get involved in the workers' cause. As for Dic himself, he is a leader, but not a demagogue: he feels deeply for the condition of his fellows but has read widely and, when it comes to it, cannot accept the violence that Lewsyn and the rest launch themselves into so eagerly.

One thing that Williams does is to return the Welsh element to the story, partly by using local colour and characters – Dic Dywyll the ballad singer, chapel meetings, Taliesin ap Iolo and his father's bardic tales, the young Edward Matthews Ewenni – but also, on a sterner note, the oppression not just of the workers, but of Wales as a country. At the end Dic says of Lewsyn, who is waiting to be transported:

> He was a good Welshman, proud of his people, and it is a wicked judgement that condemns him to be separated from his people for the rest of his life. It is only another means of achieving the one great end of the entire system which controls our lives under an English banner: the annihilation of a nation. The more our language is stifled and our people separated and estranged, the more we are destroyed.

The Angry Vineyard is something of an odd mixture. There are lyrical passages describing the natural world or Dic's home and his love for Nana, his wife, but there are also what can only be called stodgy passages of political or religious comment. And towards the close we are treated to biographical accounts of Lord Melbourne and Judge Bosanquet which add nothing very much to the book, but interrupt the build-up of tension as Dic waits to know if he is to be reprieved. Finally Lord Melbourne, failing in his tryst with the writer Mrs Caroline Norton, signs the order for Dic's execution: he may be impotent but he is not powerless. Yet despite its flaws, Williams's novel is a valuable addition to the post-mortem history of Dic Penderyn.

Most recently there have been two junior versions of Dic's story. *Dic Penderyn* by Meinir Wyn Edwards is part of a *Welsh Folk Tales* series aimed at younger children, and is a short retelling with lively illustrations. *Dic Penderyn and the Merthyr Rising* by Patrick Morgan and Anthony Bunko is a *Horrible Histories*-style version, in which the story is broken up with inserts on topics like 'What is a Davy Lamp?'

Finally for the moment, 2021 saw the premiere of a new play, *Iniquity/Camwedd*. This brought the story home to Aberafan, and was the product of a local community group led by the actor Stuart Broad, with the group taking their play to the Edinburgh Festival Fringe in summer 2022.

Official records tell us almost nothing about Richard Lewis: no baptismal record, no official account of his early life, a possibly ambiguous note of his marriage, and the legal details of his trial and execution. Nothing, in fact, to explain why his story has had such a grip on the general imagination over the years and why today – almost two hundred years after his death – he is still a subject for books and films, there are annual commemorations and there have recently been petitions to Parliament for a posthumous pardon. Tradition is something else: academics may, understandably, disregard what it has to tell us, and one does need to distinguish between legend – no grass on the grave, the thunderclap as he died – and communal remembrance. Yet the Richard Lewis who emerges from that tradition – intelligent, well-read, brave, loyal, quick to action, committed to the struggle for workers' rights, a leader among his fellows – is consistent, and he gives his own explanation for why he has been remembered.

'Lord, here is an injustice. Forgive them and me,' were his last words – worth remembering not just as a pious wish, but as a spur to action.

Appendices

THE EARLIEST PUBLISHED accounts by eyewitnesses or people who knew Dic's family background were in Welsh and mainly in sources not always easily available to the general public. Translations are therefore included here.

i ACCOUNTS OF THE EXECUTION

a) Revd Edmund Evans's account of the execution, as given to the biographer of Revd David Williams

This is an extract from a *Cofiant* (commemorative article) in the denominational journal *Eurgrawn Wesleyaidd*.

> The comments about Revd D Williams himself have been included to give a flavour of the thinking of these men, the last to speak to Dic before he died.
>
> [David Williams's] judgement was mature, his godliness deep, and he was compelling in prayer, when he applied himself to any cause relating to his office as a man of God; and certain things that happened prove this, and among them the following. We do not follow him this time to a great meeting, to listen to entertaining pleasantries; nor to the 'Society' [combination prayer meeting/confessional] to listen to him discussing the condition of the Christian life; nor to the sickbed of a 'saint' who was taking wing for a better world;

but to the prison, to the condemned man under sentence of death. In the first year of the three during which he was on the circuit, i.e. 1831, a riot broke out in Merthyr Tydfil and the surrounding districts; and among those of the rioters who were arrested and imprisoned in Cardiff was one by the name of Richard Lewis, or, as he was commonly called, Dic Penderyn, who had been sentenced to be executed. Mr Williams and his two fellow-workers went to see the wretched man, and that several times. Our late comrade Edmund Evans was on that circuit at that time. Mr Evans gave an account of two very effective visits. The day before the execution, the two went to the prison 'and', said brother Evans, 'Mr Williams asked the condemned man some questions about the matter of his soul. Then [Dic] said that he hoped that God would have pity on him, and would show in some way that he was not guilty of stabbing the soldier. "Richard *bach*," said Mr Williams, "I am not asking anything about that, but I wish to be honest with you, because you are going to face the all-knowing God; and it would be a terrible thing for you to meet Him with a lie on your lips." "Indeed it would," he said then, "but I am not guilty." They prayed with him, with painful emotions, and counselled him to seek mercy from God, through Jesus Christ.

'On the morning of Saturday, August 13th, at 6 o'clock in the morning, Mr Williams went there again, with his fellow-worker, Mr Jones, and the priest; and at 7 o'clock, Mr Rowlands and I [Edmund Evans] arrived to join them. The priest was at prayer, and after he had finished, I prayed, then Mr Williams, with such compulsion and earnestness that one might expect the heavens to open. We went to the chapel of the gaol to take the sacrament and the Lord's Supper, while we were in floods of tears. At that point someone came to bind him and lead him to the scaffold. After that solemn task, we moved – the sheriff and the keeper of the gaol first – then the priest, reading the burial service – next after that the prisoner, between Mr Williams and the executioner; and last. Messrs Jones, Rowlands and myself.'

But in conversation brother Edmund Evans gave a much fuller and more detailed description of the wisdom, suitability and application of the ministry of the object of our biography in these oppressive circumstances. He himself tried to describe the circumstances to the writer but on beginning the story, the gravity of the event rose up before his eyes, and overcame him, so that he was only able to say a very little of what went on in the silence.

b) An extract from the biography of Revd Edmund Evans

As with the previous section, this is an extract from a *Cofiant* in the *Eurgrawn Wesleyaidd*.

After completing his task in the Merthyr Circuit [Revd Edmund Evans] turned his attention to the Cardiff Circuit; and there he underwent one of the most moving experiences of his life. It is from the man himself that we know this. We will give an account of this now.

On the second of June 1831, a terrible riot broke out in Merthyr Tydfil. A host of miners, and some other workers, congregated together and then went together from place to place to riot, to plunder and to destroy. Next day there was a severe battle between them and the soldiers in front of the Castle Inn in the 'village' of Merthyr, as it was called at that time. During that morning, before the battle started, 'it happened that some rash scoundrel broke out saying that the soldiers had come there to defend persons and their property; and if everyone did as he would do, they would take their weapons from them; and it would be the worse for him if he was not the first to try it; and with that he jumped off the shoulders of those who were carrying him, and the rioters snatched the weapons from the front row [of the soldiers], about thirty in number, and a fearful conflict took place.'

The name of this bold 'scoundrel' was Lewis Lewis, or
Lewis the Huntsman. During the 'fearful conflict' that followed
his brave, but very foolish attack, one of the soldiers was
wounded, and one Richard Lewis, or 'Dic Penderyn', was
arrested on the charge of wounding him. He denied that he
was guilty of the crime, but he and Lewis yr Heliwr were
taken as prisoners to Cardiff, the chief town of the county.
After a serious and deliberate trial, the two transgressors
were condemned to death. Through the vigorous endeavours
of Mr Price of Neath Abbey, Lewis Lewis's life was spared,
but Richard Lewis was left to die; and offering support to
this wretched man was the moving experience to which we
referred. We will relate the rest [of the story] in his own words.
For the benefit of the reader, we explain that the Revds David
Williams, T Jones and W Rowlands were working on the
Cardiff Welsh Circuit; also that the Revd D Williams was living
in Trelai, or as most people call it now, 'Ely', a pretty little
country place near Cardiff. Now we take the story from the
diary of Revd Edmund Evans.

Friday 12th [August 1831]. I visited Mr Williams in Trelai.
I went with Mr Williams to the gaol in Cardiff to visit the
prisoner who was going to perish because of some riot there
had been in Merthyr; and we found him crying and in tears. O
solemn hours! We counselled him, and prayed with him, and
then prayed together. But his thoughts were imprisoned by the
feeling he had suffered injustice. Messrs Jones and Rowlands
went to him in the afternoon to pray with him.

Saturday 13th. A dark and cloudy day. At five in the
morning we went to the town [Cardiff], to the prisoner, and
found him with the chaplain praying with him. I prayed after
him, and the prisoner was very fervent with us. The day before
we had exhorted him to ask 'for Jesus' sake'; for he had no idea
of the Mediator/Intercessor. After me Mr D Williams took his
turn to pray; and I never heard prayer like that; it was as if he
was opening heaven from man to man. After that the Gaoler
came, with a cup of tea for him, and a thin slice of bread and
butter, but he took no food; he drank the cup of tea and that

was all. Then his wife came, to say goodbye to him. O, it was impossible for any heart to witness that without breaking! I hope I will never again see anything like that.

We went to the place where they usually read the service, and we took communion from the hand of Mr Jones, the chaplain, and the prisoner with us. There were four of us there, Williams, Jones, Rowlands and I. Rowlands and Jones went to pray, and last of all the prisoner prayed, very fervently. Then the chaplain read some verses from the Psalms; and in the middle of that the clock struck eight! And it was time to begin! Out we went to the 'court'. With that, the executioner came forward, binding his arms with a rope, and the keeper of the gaol put fetters on his hands. He cried out, 'O, here is injustice.' We went on, behind the prisoner, onto the scaffold, to see thousands of spectators. O, what a fearful sight! The chaplain read the burial service, and then, while the executioner was putting the rope round his neck, the poor man sent a piercing shout echoing across the whole town, 'O, here is injustice. O Jesus, forgive them and me.' Then the trapdoor opened and he was gone into the presence of the great Judge. We turned our backs; and went, together, to the place where we had taken the sacrament, and went down on our knees, the five of us, Mr Jones the chaplain, and we four. Then we went down to see the other prisoner (Lewsyn yr Heliwr), who had also been condemned at one point, but was to be transported instead. He was crying out a great deal after his fellow prisoner, and said many times, "Indeed, he didn't do it," meaning the wounding of the soldier, "no, indeed; I know who did do it; but I will never tell anyone." O fearful day!'

NOTE

The four ministers were Wesleyan Methodists. Earlier there had been Baptist and Independent ministers there, all presumably fulfilling Bosanquet's order that the condemned men should have full spiritual support to prepare themselves for judgement after death. Edmund Evans had previously been based in the

Merthyr area, but seems to have moved to Cardiff before the riots; it was his denomination's custom to move ministers every three years. It would seem that the four saw Dic as an ignorant workman with no knowledge of the Scriptures, who was too busy denying his guilt to attend to his soul. They felt some pity for the condemned man but, one suspects, were too concerned with their own feelings to understand the quality of the man they were there to support. In fairness, possibly actual executions were by then comparatively rare, which may be one reason why the four men found the experience so difficult to cope with – one has to remember the authorities' difficulty in finding a hangman.

ii ACCOUNT OF THE FUNERAL

This account comes from an article in *Y Drysorfa*, lxxxix, 1919, pp.418–19. *Y Drysorfa* was a monthly magazine published by the Calvinistic Methodist denomination, to which Dic's family and the Revd Morgan Howells, his brother-in-law, belonged. Although the title and article refer to a letter, it seems to be more of a report of an interview.

An Interesting Old Letter

In the middle of the year 1831 there took place one of the most harmful strikes ever to occur in the industrial regions of South Wales. Wages at the time were very low and the necessities of life were expensive and scarce, especially for the very poor. Among the workers there was a man called Richard Lewis, 'Dic Penderyn' – a man of more than common ability, and a sufficiently blameless character. He was one of those most forward in debating workers' rights, and drew many black looks from the masters for daring to defend the poor in the face of the oppressions that bore them to the ground. Thousands stayed out in the Merthyr Tydfil area and they saw before long that events were looking ominous and no one knew what would happen the next moment. Soldiers were sent there to keep the peace, but their arrival set the workers on fire. The Redcoats clashed with the black coats, and in the great battle over twenty workers were murdered, among them girls and women. Some of the soldiers were also murdered. Several [of the workers] were taken to prison, among them Richard Lewis. He was condemned to death and the rest were sentenced to imprisonment. Lewis swore to the end that he was completely innocent, and that was the opinion of the countryside at the time, especially those who knew him. But all the force and influence of the masters was against him, and nothing would please them but to put him out of the way. Some years after the unjust sentence had been carried out, another man confessed that he had murdered the soldier and that Dic Penderyn was as innocent as a dove.

The letter was written years ago, during an interview with an old man, over eighty years of age, who remembered the circumstances very well. We are publishing it out of respect for the memory of an innocent man and on account of the reference in it to that fiery old preacher, Morgan Howells.

Here is the letter:

'Richard Lewis – Dic Penderyn – was the son of Lewis Lewis, who lived in a little place called Penderyn, in Pyle. He had another brother called John Lewis, 'John the Lime-man'. He was there for years, burning lime, and the ruins of the old building can still be seen today at Cefncribwr.

"And did you see him being hanged?"

"Yes, I saw Dic Penderyn being hanged, August 13 1831, on Saturday morning, in Cardiff town. Yes, truly, I did. I saw Dic coming out through the little gate and climbing onto the scaffold. And then he said, 'O Lord, here is an injustice.' There were thousands of men there from every part of the country. Morgan Howells had been appointed to preach under the drop, but he refused."

"Why did Morgan Howells concern himself with it?"

"Dic's sister was Morgan Howells's first wife. When

Dic had been hanging for the required time, thunder and lightning broke out, and it rained terribly. At nine o'clock the body was moved, and we went with it to the Prince Regent in Crockherbtown (one of the main streets in Cardiff). After taking the body to the Prince Regent, it was put in another coffin, and the coffin got from the jail was used as a shell for this."

"How did you come to go to Cardiff, when you were only a young lad at the time?"

"Well, I'll tell you. On Thursday afternoon a letter came from Dic's relations, from Cardiff, announcing that he was going to be hanged on the following Saturday morning, and asking the neighbours to be kind enough to offer help in bringing the body to be buried in Aberafan. The news ran like wildfire through the neighbourhood. My grandfather cut short his labour when the news came, and they stopped working there, and everybody who was in the field went sorrowfully towards their homes. During the Friday the farmers gathered together to go to Cardiff and bring the body back with them. There were about thirty or more gambos driving towards Cardiff that day, and hundreds of men walking. They reached Cardiff about six o'clock on Saturday morning, and stayed there throughout the day until Saturday night.

'They set off with the body about 6 o'clock on Sunday morning, through St Nicholas, and when they got there, there was a huge crowd of men from Cowbridge who had come to meet them; and when they got to Cowbridge, the men from Bridgend had come in hosts; and the men from Pyle to Bridgend and the men from Aberafan in one swarm to Pyle, to meet with the body and the family. It was a huge funeral. It was late in the afternoon when we reached Aberafan. The priest read the service as he would have read it for any other man. He was buried near the churchyard wall – there were only six graves between his grave and the wall, and it had a flat stone on it when I saw it later. We didn't go into the church at all. The body was moved from the gambo to the grave, and after the priest had finished the usual funeral service, Morgan Howells got up from outside the churchyard wall and addressed the enormous crowd in front of him. The first thing he said was, "Dic, lad, are you there? You were not afraid of the rope"; and he spoke until we were all beside ourselves.

'Dic did not eat a morsel of anything while he was in jail after receiving the sentence. He was from a very religious family, and was a moral young man, though not himself a believer. He had considerable ability and knew more about history and the affairs of the world than any other worker of that time. The masters were afraid of him. It is likely that Ianto Parker was the murderer and Lewsyn yr Helwr (sic) incited the crowd to rush at the soldiers.'

This is the old letter, and we believe that what it remembers and preserves merits being brought to the light of day. The old ballad singer Dic Dywyll sang a song on the occasion, and this is in complete agreement with the details of the story in the letter, but there is much more of a story in this old letter than there is poetry in the ballad. It can be seen that the old letter corrects another mistake. The general idea is that Dic got his nickname from the village of Penderyn, near Hirwaun. This is a mistake. He was a native of the borders of the Vale of Glamorgan, and that is why his dust lies there after he had been wrongfully murdered by the law of the land.

NOTES

1   The Merthyr Rising grew out of a combination of moves towards parliamentary reform and general social and economic unrest, rather than from a strike.

2   Soldiers were injured, but none were killed. As discussed previously, Donald Black, the soldier Dic was found guilty of stabbing, was sufficiently recovered to give evidence at the trial – where he could not identify his attacker.

3   John Lewis, Dic's brother, lived at Pyle. Possibly Dic's father also lived there after leaving Merthyr, or he may already have died. There is no mention of him at the time of the trial. John and his family continued to live at Pyle,

where Morgan Howells visited them in later years. Dic's own links were with Aberafan, but perhaps it was John's residence at Pyle that led to any confusion.

4 According to family history, Morgan Howells rode to England to ask for a royal pardon, but was unsuccessful. If this is true, his absence would explain a number of points, particularly the delay in starting for Aberafan.

5 It was a grey, drizzly morning. Dic's body was left hanging for an hour, no doubt as an awful warning to anyone tempted to rebel against authority. The thunderstorm that broke out during this time was later transformed to a clap of thunder at the moment of execution.

6 Crockherbtown is now Queen Street.

7 This was presumably the sequel to the letter Dic wrote to his sister, making arrangements for the disposal of his body and saying goodbye to his family. It has to be said that this businesslike way of dealing with his own death and his bearing on the scaffold suggest that the Revd Edmund Evans and the other ministers rather over-emphasised their picture of the repentant sinner in floods of tears.

8 We are not told where the old man lived, but it was most likely to have been Aberafan or Margam. It took his party all of Friday night to reach Cardiff.

9 A gambo was a farm cart.

10 As mentioned earlier, possibly these relays of mourners from the towns and villages along the route were the origin of the story that Dic's body was refused burial by all the churches along the way. Aberafan was, in fact, always the intended destination.

11 The old St Mary's Church would have been too small and dilapidated for such a large crowd. The curate was evidently sympathetic, as can be seen from his note in the parish register about 'this unfortunate man'.

12 The present grave cannot be described as 'near the churchyard wall', and there are six pre-1831 tombstones between it and the wall, so it was evidently not the wall that was moved. It is possible that the body was reburied later, in a place of greater honour or nearer to his family, perhaps when the church was rebuilt in 1857–9. The gravestone to the left of Dic's monument is for an Elizabeth Jenkins and her children – whether this is significant is not known, but she would have been of an age to be Dic's grandmother or great-aunt.

13 To say that Dic was not a 'believer' does not necessarily mean that he was either an atheist or a non-chapelgoer, simply that he was not a fully enrolled member of his denomination. Chapel membership was a very serious matter in those days, and there were faithful followers, known as *gwrandawyr,* who contributed time and money to the cause, but never felt worthy of membership. One, from Aberafan, walked all the way to north Wales and back in the late nineteenth century to raise funds to build a new chapel. Dic's recorded words in the last few days of his life make it clear that belief was important to him.

14 It is interesting to note that those involved in the procession from Cardiff were apparently the farmers of the Vale, not the workers of Merthyr. No doubt the latter were still understandably afraid of reprisals – even some 50 or so years later Isaac Evans and the anonymous correspondent in *Y Drysorfa* seemed wary about saying too much on the matter. What is surprising is that the farmers of the Vale were willing to give up at least three full days in high summer to go and collect the body of a convicted felon from Cardiff. There was clearly something more going on here than we can now appreciate.

iii LETTERS TO THE PRESS

a) Account of meeting the man who stabbed the soldier (*Tarian y Gweithiwr*, 31 July 1884)

Tarian y Gweithiwr was a weekly Welsh-language newspaper published in Aberdare. The name of the author of this first letter to the paper is not given, but the piece is at the end of a column of news about Welsh Americans.

Memories of the wrongful execution of Dic Penderyn: the murderer escaped to America

I was only a little lad when Dic Penderyn was executed, but although I was so small, the circumstances with regard to the opinion of the public about the injustice and unfairness of the court that convicted Dic has stayed alive in my memory as fresh as if it had happened recently. Everyone who knew anything about that story knows that it was through the false witness of a man called Abbott, a barber, and one of the toadies of the big men of the day, that Dic, poor soul, was executed. This Abbott observed that it happened that Dic was definitely in the crowd; and because Dic was very prominent in claiming his rights in those days, the oppressors and tyrants judged that they could put him out of the way, to their own advantage. This would allow them to carry out their own arrogant and inhuman intentions, and it is certain that the fact that Dic was in the crowd was enough for the wretch Abbott to swear an oath that Dic had committed the deed of killing the soldier. This was also enough to make that same oath acceptable to the court, which was made up of greedy men ready to push away over the precipice of oblivion every objection that arose in their unjust path, in order to frighten everyone thereafter from asking for their rights.

The witness on oath of that soldier, in addition to Abbott, did not agree with that of the court. [This was apparently not a reference to Donald Black – if another soldier *did* give evidence in court, that was not recorded.] He gave witness that

the person who had killed his fellow soldier had lost his ear
through his own sword, and he was the person who should
be punished, not Dic, because Dic's ears were whole when
he was executed. In order to prove the truth of that soldier's
testimony, I can say that I met the person who committed the
deed for which Dic was executed in St Clair, Pennsylvania,
about the year 1854. He showed me the wound caused by the
soldier's sword, which had cut his ear away, and told me how
he had escaped from Wales to France, and having lived there
for some years, emigrated to the United States. He felt sad that
Dic, poor soul, had had to suffer the most extreme punishment
of the law; he also felt deeply for the unfortunate soldier who
had fallen as a sacrifice under his own hand in the struggle,
but in the circumstances it was either he himself or the soldier
who must fall. This was after the man known as Lewsyn yr
Heliwr had climbed up the lamp-post by the Angel Inn [sic]
and shouted, "If you are of the same mind as me, rush through
them!" (He meant the soldiers who were guarding the Angel
Inn [sic], the headquarters of the soldiers and the refuge of the
cruel oppressors who were terrified by the threatening attitude
of the excited crowd outside, until they could be delivered
behind the power of the military.) The people at the back [of
the crowd] were crushed against those at the front until they
clashed with the soldiers and were caught up with them. In
that collision the soldier fell and the man who felled him lost
his ear, but escaped for his life overseas, and the result of this
was that Dic, poor soul, because he was in the crowd and was
a prominent man, was, through the false witness of the barber
Abbott, condemned and suffered the most extreme penalty of
the law, although he was completely innocent. He suffered the
punishment although no one had discovered who the person
was who carried out the act. I could give the name of the
man of whom I speak, but I believe it would be unwise and
inappropriate to do that at the present time.

Although he was alive in 1831, the writer of this letter was too
young to have been present during the riots – he is reporting

what he has heard. He gets the name of the Castle Inn wrong, but otherwise his account seems to be reasonably correct.

b) Isaac Evans's letter
(*Tarian y Gweithiwr*, 14 August 1884)

Two weeks after the preceding letter, *Tarian y Gweithiwr* published a response from Isaac Evans – nephew of Dic's friend John Evans, who married Dic's widow. He confirms the accuracy of the bulk of what the previous correspondent had written: their only real point of disagreement is whether Dic was present in the crowd at the Castle Inn. In fact both may be correct. Dic *was* in front of the Castle Inn before the attack took place, but not after the deputation came out of the inn.

Dic Penderyn and the 'Castle' riots

I read the piece in the *Tarian* dated 31 July, about the execution of Dic Penderyn. It related the truth as far as the author was aware of it, and it was good to read what he had to say. As far as I know, he only made one mistake, that is in saying that Abbott saw [Dic] in the crowd. I do not say this in order to criticise the author, but to do justice to Richard's character. It is a definite fact that Dic Penderyn was not near the crowd at all; and to prove this I think it is my duty to make public the story as I had it from a companion of Dic Penderyn, one who was with him in flight from the *rioters* on the slopes of Aberdare Mountain. This companion was my uncle, my father's brother, the one who married Dic Penderyn's widow a few years after his execution and had two children with her, a boy and a girl. The boy died, but the girl, who is deaf and dumb, is alive now and living in Merthyr. Her present name is Elizabeth Richards, from her husband, but her maiden name was Elizabeth Evans, from her father (John Evans), my uncle. Richard's last letter (written the night before his execution) to his wife is at the moment in the possession of my uncle, and I have read it myself. The letter was printed and a number of copies sold to support his widow, who is now dead, and my uncle John Evans was her second husband.

This is the story that I had from my uncle: 'Dic Penderyn was a man full of life, one who was well-grown and good looking, and possessed of strength and skill in his fists, a hard worker, but too fond at times of strong drink. It happened that there was a fight between him and Shoni Crydd, who was also good with his fists, and was also a [parish] constable; but Dic struck him and that caused suspicion in the other constables who were with Shoni Crydd against Dic, poor lad. And when the riots broke out, he was afraid that they would accuse him among the first when they had an opportunity to do this, and so the unfortunate Dic Penderyn got ready to keep away in the hiding places of Aberdare Mountain until it got late and the bloody business by the Castle Inn in Merthyr had calmed down. My uncle went home before he did; but Richard, poor lad, waited, in case the constables saw him and took him up in error, and when it was about ten or eleven o'clock, he went home. But the constables had been looking for him before he got in; and when they learned that he was not at home, then that caused more ill-feeling. The constables were looking for the *rioters*. They came back a second time, and took Dic Penderyn, poor soul, in his bed, and he was held on suspicion and taken that night to the 'Dark House' (there was no police station to be found at that time). There the unprincipled Abbott testified against him (as the writer in the *Tarian* of 31 July mentioned); and he was made to mount the scaffold and face eternity, although totally innocent of that of which he had been convicted.'

Isaac Evans then discusses the causes of the riots – the Court of Requests, etc. He says he does not accuse the authorities of the evils that came from the courts, but rather the greedy, unjust men who staffed them. ['I do not shame the authorities in the slightest.'] He describes how the shopkeepers could get writs for six or seven shillings or less, but that the bailiffs would seize something worth £20 or £30 to pay for a few shillings. 'At that time the bums would seize things even from the arms of the women, holding them so that they could not leave, while the others carried the furniture far enough away, especially if the house was by itself without any neighbours, and that, perhaps, for nothing more than a pot. That was the main cause of the riots.'

Evans then goes on to describe the events leading up to the riot in front of the Castle Inn. Then he discusses how his father, who was a member with the Baptists and a deacon in Seion, Twynyrodyn, and his father's friend William Morla, 'formerly of Rhydycar, Merthyr', were caught within ropes being held by the rioters advancing towards Hirwaun to meet the cavalry, and forced to go along with them. Isaac's father managed to dodge away into an old level at Gellideg where he had once worked, but the crowd chased after him, pulled down the mouth of the level and left him shut inside. Meanwhile William Morla was carried along with the crowd until he managed to excuse himself 'because he needed to turn aside for a little, and he would follow them like a stout fellow.' After he had waited to one side for a moment and could see that the crowd was far enough away, he went back to the level and opened it up so that Isaac's father could get out.

> That was a troubled time for all those who loved peace. I was only a little more than two years old at the time, and I was living with my father and mother at the crossroads leading to Ynysgau and the iron bridge over the River Taf, or the Glebelands, Merthyr. I remember hearing my mother tell how there was no one in the house but herself and four children, and the door was fastened. The oldest of us was only seven and the youngest three months. At that point my father had fled, to hide himself in the barn of Penylan Farm, near the Graig Farm, Merthyr. She gathered us together upstairs and looked out into the road. When she heard the sound of

cannon thundering in her ears, she saw a Scottish soldier whose face was covered in blood, with some five or six of the rioters hitting him with clubs and trampling his headgear and plumage in the gutter. The soldier ran to the crossroads that leads towards the River Morlais and a Scottish townsman from Merthyr opened the door to him, warning him to jump inside for his life. He lost his pursuers, who had no idea where he had gone, and so he saved his life.

My father died of the cholera that broke out after the riots, and my mother was left to bring us up alone, which she did nobly, and she is worthy of respectful memory.

William Morla of Rhydycar died a few years ago. He was a man fond of a drink, but he never did wrong to anyone, as I know.

I will end with that, hoping that nothing I have said will harm anyone whatsoever.

46 Penrhiwceiber, Isaac Evans

NOTES

1   Dic's letter to his wife, which Isaac had seen but regrettably did not quote, was clearly not the same as the letter sent to his sister a day or so before, asking for his body to be taken to Aberafan. He may not have known that they would be allowed one final meeting on the morning of his execution.

2   Although Isaac does not mention anything more than Dic's fight with Shoni Crydd as a motive for the constables going to arrest him, the fact that Dic, Isaac's father and his uncle all went into hiding suggests that there may have been something else involved. One might speculate that the three men were an active part of the incipient union movement, known to the authorities as such, and so a target – and that this was why, even 50-odd years later, those writing about the event were still wary of saying too much.

iv LEWIS DAVIES, *YSTORIAU SILURIA*

Lewis Davies was a teacher in Cymmer in the Afan Valley. He had clearly picked up some of the local traditions about Dic, but here he is following the official line about the execution. Thus, though he acknowledges Dic's bravery and steadfastness, he paints him as a young hooligan and assumes, as many did then and have since, that the soldier was killed. Davies's book (published in 1921) is aimed at children – probably mainly boys – and so Dic becomes an awful warning about wasted talent and bad behaviour.

A few yards from the door of St Mary's Church, Aberafan, lies a stone that reminds us of one of the most exciting stories of south Wales.

The description on the stone, now almost unreadable, is 'R. I. 1831', and it is said that under it lies all that was mortal of Dic Penderyn (Richard Lewis).

He was a native of Aberafan (despite the nickname 'Penderyn') and it is said that he was, when a lad, always full of life and energy, and dissatisfied if he was not the leader in every game. He rarely went to school, and when he was there, his old schoolmaster was often forced to warn him to put a bridle on his fiery temper.

Dic did not remember his mother, but he had a sister, Gwen, who took great care of him. Like the schoolmaster, she tried to lead Dic away from his foolhardy path, but she did not succeed, and he continued to be a trouble and a care.

One of his sudden furies was the cause of his leaving his home, because in a quarrel between him and Dafi Cound, Taibach, about playing bando, he pushed Dafi over a steep wall at the harbour into the sea below.

The next second Dic jumped after him to try to rescue the boy, although only a moment before, in his foolish temper, he had pushed him down.

It might well have been that the worst lesson for the two

162

would have been a wetting, but alas for Dafi, when he fell into the water, he struck against the big beam at the bottom of the embankment and so broke his back. Dic was terrified by what he had done, and because he was suffering from pangs of remorse, he fled to Merthyr.

That town was a Mecca for all Welsh pilgrims at the time, and there, too, came 'Dic like a bird' from Aberafan, to become 'Dic Penderyn' in the new place, known to everyone as one of the bravest, but also one of the most unruly boys in the area.

If Dic's bravery had been well directed, it may be that we would read about him now as a hero, and not as an evil-doer and lawbreaker.

In Merthyr he became friends with a man older than himself called Lewsyn the Huntsman, originally a native, oddly enough, of Penderyn, the little village on the borders of Breconshire, near Hirwaun.

Merthyr was very turbulent at that time, and Lewsyn was the idol of the multitude and a leader in every commotion between the disorderly youth of the place and the keepers of the peace.

In all these skirmishes there was no one more faithful to their leader than Dic. He was at his side when they forced the captain of the cavalry from Swansea to yield up his sword to the Huntsman from Penderyn on Aberdare Mountain. He too, with other men, let loose a shower of stones down Cilsanws mountain across the cavalry from Brecon who were trying to reach Merthyr from the north.

But the greatest combat between the unruly Welsh and the Scottish soldiers was fought out in front of the Castle Hotel in Merthyr High Street, and it was because of their part in this that Lewsyn and Dic were condemned to death.

The mob gathered, enraged by hunger and unafraid because of their previous successes, in one crowd in front of the famous old inn.

After they had arranged themselves in a single rank on the pavement, with their backs to the wall, the purpose of the Scottish Highlanders was to endeavour to keep the doors and lower windows of the hotel clear while Mr Crawshay and the other ironmasters addressed the crowd.

At the moment when the workers were being advised to return peacefully to their homes, behold Lewsyn leaping up furiously and then, shouting 'Blood or Bread', seizing a musket from the soldier next to him and stabbing him with his own bayonet.

The street was like a battleground for the next half hour, with the Welshmen trying to rush on the soldiers and the latter – brave lads every one – vigorously pushing them back from climbing into the inn.

At that point one could see the mistake made in putting the single rank on the pavement at all, and the very hard task they had now to get out of there in the face of the anger of the crowd. They all had to run, one by one, for their lives, past the corner of the house, to get to the door of the large yard of the inn in the side road.

There, to stop them from reaching safety, was Dic Penderyn, with some of the most determined of his men.

But despite that, the Scots reached safety, all except for the last.

This one showed the most bravery of all of them, and on him fell all the anger of the attackers. He was beaten unmercifully, but he continued to fight in spite of all his wounds.

In the end he was running to try to gain the safety of the great door; but when he reached that spot, there were Dic Penderyn and two or three others, hanging on his flanks like bloodhounds trying to drag down a wounded lion.

We do not know more of what happened behind the big door, but the brave soldier was dead and Dic was accused of causing his death.

In the trial that followed the sad events, Lewsyn and Dic were condemned to suffer death, but before the sentence was carried out, Lewsyn's penalty was commuted to punishment for life. Dic, poor soul, was hanged, although he insisted that he was innocent until the end.

In those days the family of anyone hanged had the sad right to bury the remains of their relative. Dic's brother claimed this favour. He borrowed a farmer's cart, and travelling overnight bore his brother's body through the Vale of Glamorgan at every step from Cardiff to Aberafan by the following afternoon.

The funeral was remarkably large, although Dic had been condemned in his country's court, and it was apparent that he came from respectable stock, and more than that, the ordinary people believed that he was steadfast although he was hanged for doing wrong.

All the burial service he had was the singing of a Welsh hymn – given out, it is said, by his old teacher, David Jones [sic], the schoolmaster of Aberafan.

v DIC'S LAST LETTER

It is not until the last few days of his life that we can hear Dic's own voice. His words are firm and to the point, denying any guilt and hoping that his innocence will in some way be made known – something that happily, most of all for his family, did come to pass.

> *Yr wyf yn deisyf arnat i ddyfod yn ddiatreg i hol fy nghorff, oherwydd nid oes dim tebygolrwydd am ddim arall yn bresennol. Dos at Phillip Lewis a gwna iddo ef ddyfod a chertyn i lawr heno, a chymaint o ddynion a allo, mewn rhyw wedd, i ddyfod gydag ef. Yr wyf yn credu fod yr Arglwydd wedi maddau i fi fy amrywiol bechodau a'm troseddiadau, ond am yr hyn yr wyf yn nawr yn cael fy nghyhuddio nid yr wyf yn euog; am hynny mae gennyf achos i fod yn ddiolchgar.*

I ask you to come without delay to fetch my body as there is no likelihood of anything else at present. Go to Phillip Lewis and get him to come down with a cart tonight somehow, and as many men as he can manage. I believe that the Lord has forgiven me my many sins and transgressions, but of that of which I am accused, I am not guilty, and for that I have reason to be thankful.

Dic is said to have written/dictated three things in those last few days: a hymn, a letter to his wife and a note to his sister, concerning the disposal of his body. The hymn is mentioned by D Emrys Lewis, along with the handcuffs which were kept by the family of the High Sheriff, but it seems to have been lost. The letter to his wife ended up in the possession of John Evans, Dic's friend and his wife's second husband, where Isaac Evans saw it. If it was, as Isaac says, printed to raise funds for Dic's widow, then there may still be copies to be found.

The note first appears in print in a letter from Martin Phillips to the *Western Mail* on 23 February 1933, sent after he had received a copy from an E G Morris of 10 Vivian Terrace, Aberafan. The copy includes another two sentences expressing Dic's pious wishes for his relatives, friends and enemies and for himself, but Phillips seems not to have seen these as relevant because he did not include them when providing a copy of the note for the press or for Islwyn ap Nicholas, and his version has come to be seen as standard.

The note is addressed to *Fy annwyl Chwaer* (My dear sister) and is dated 11 August, which fits the old man's statement reported in *Y Drysorfa* that the news reached Aberafan on the Thursday afternoon.

It ends:

Fy annwyl Chwaer a fy mherthnasau, fy nghyfeillion oll a fy ngelynion, gweddiwch i Dduw eich cadw oddi wrth bob drwg rhag i chwi ddyfod i'r un bwlch cyfyng. Felly, byddwch wych, a gobeithiwn am gael cyfarfod yn y Nefoedd tu Iesu Grist [fu] farw o farwolaeth y groes i achub pechaduriaid, ac yr wyf yn credu y bydd iddo fy achub innau y pennaf ohonynt. Unwaith yn rhagor byddwch wych.

My dear Sister and my relatives, all my friends and my enemies, pray to God to keep you from all evil lest you come to the same narrow pass. Therefore, fare thee well and let us hope to be allowed to meet in the heavens beside Jesus Christ, who died the death of the cross to save sinners, and I believe he will save me, the greatest of them all. Once more, fare thee well.

Endnotes

CHAPTER 1: Early Years

1   *Y Drysorfa*, 1919, lxxxix, pp.418–19
2   *Western Mail*, 3 March 1933. This was a letter from James Evans; he also wrote to the *Western Mail* on 19 May 1947, and in *The Merthyr Rising* Gwyn A Williams notes another letter that Evans sent to Professor David Williams, dated 11 May 1949.
3   Morgan, E, *Boanerges*, p.62
4   Williams, G A, *The Merthyr Rising*, pp.173–4
5   *Rhondda Leader*, 29 March 1990, p.3; Meredith, I, 'Dic Penderyn's family' in *Glamorgan Family History Society Journal*, June 1998; Isaac Evans, *Tarian y Gweithiwr*, 14 August 1884
6   Jones, Helen, 'The Search for Dic Penderyn' in *GFHS*, March 1998, and letters in the author's possession
7   Sue Thomas, letter of 4 July 1997, in the author's possession.
8   Information from A L Evans
9   Jenkins, C, *All Against the Collar*, p.12
10 The grave next to Dic's in St Mary's churchyard is of the Jenkins family. Elizabeth Jenkins was of an age to be Dic's grandmother, though her daughter Mary – also named – would have been too young to be Dic's mother.
11 Donovan, Edward, *Descriptive Excursions through South Wales and Monmouthshire in the year 1804 and the*

preceding four summers (self-published, 1805), Vol. 2, pp.45–7

12   Islwyn ap Nicholas, *Dic Penderyn*, p.12
13   Davies, Lewis, *Ystoriau Siluria*, pp.69–70. The story is also in Islwyn ap Nicholas, pp.12–13. One local source for this information would have been Martin Phillips, a member of the Aberafan and Margam Historical Society and author of several articles on local industrial history.
14   Davies, p.69
15   Matthews, Edward, *Siencyn Penhydd*, trans. A L Evans, 1989, pp.41–2
16   Nicholas, John, *Yr Hen Ddyffryn*, p.166
17   Ibid., pp.30–7
18   Ibid., pp.60–1
19   These were rescued when the old Carmel was demolished in 1973. The chapel clearly had an extensive library.
20   Information from Sir Geoffrey Howe
21   Helen Jones, letter in the author's possession
22   Islwyn ap Nicholas, p.12. The dates given tally with those for Dafydd Rees's Sunday School at Carmel.
23   Isaac Evans, *Tarian y Gweithiwr*, 14 August 1884

CHAPTER 2: Over to Merthyr

1   Williams, G A, 'The Merthyr of Dic Penderyn' in *Merthyr Politics*, pp.9–27
2   Cliffe, C F, *The Book of South Wales*, p.129
3   Williams, *Merthyr Politics*, pp.12–13
4   Davies, p.69
5   William, E, *Rhyd-y-car*, pp.2–6. In his letter in *Tarian y Gweithiwr*, 14 August 1884, Isaac Evans speaks of his father's friend, William Morla, formerly of Rhyd-y-car.
6   *Westminster Review*, quoted in Thomas, H, *Cyffro Cymdeithas yng Nghymru, 1800–1843*, p.27
7   Helen Jones, letter in the author's possession
8   Islwyn ap Nicholas, p.13

9   Williams, *The Merthyr Rising*, p.173

10 Morgan, E, p.41

11 James Evans's letter, *Western Mail*, 30 March 1933. It should be noted that after Elizabeth Howells died young, Morgan married again and then died fairly young himself, leaving their daughters to be brought up by the second wife. Hence the connection with Dic was not often spoken about, and he was remembered as a 'wild young man' – not morally, but politically.

12 Cordell, A, *Requiem for a Patriot*, p.11. Information from Hugh Jones.

13 Information from Steffan ap Dafydd

14 Islwyn ap Nicholas, p.14

15 *Y Drysorfa*. pp.418–19

16 Meredith, I, *Glamorgan Family History Society*, June 1998; *Rhondda Leader*, 29 March 1990. p.3. At a recent conference on Anglo-Welsh literature I met Bethan Jenkins, a descendant of the Rhondda Evanses, who told me that Elizabeth Harries-Evans's daughter had been known in the family as 'Lizzie Deaf and Dumb'.

17 Jones, David, *Before Rebecca*. In *The Merthyr Rising*, Gwyn A Williams concentrates on the events of the spring and summer of 1831 and does not include the prehistory of unrest in Merthyr.

Chapter 3: Riots and Risings

1   This event is mentioned in both of Tregelles Price's petitions (see Chapter 5). Interestingly, the inference is that Abbott struck Dic, though both were then scuffling. Abbott denied being there when questioned and brought witnesses to support this, though one of them said Abbott could have been there.

2   I asked David Jones if the Thomas Llewellyn of Merthyr was also the Thomas Llewellyn of the Chartist attack on Newport, but he had not come across any connection.

3   Isaac Evans, *Tarian y Gweithiwr*, 14 August 1884

4   Gwyn A Williams in *The Merthyr Rising* (passim) and David Jones in *Before Rebecca* (pp.133–158) both give detailed accounts of the riots/Rising. It was Williams who chose the name 'Rising' – understandably, because what happened was clearly more than an outbreak of hooliganism. However, though events following the shooting outside the Castle Inn had a definite degree of organisation, it is unlikely that they were pre-planned as the Chartist attack on Newport was to be.

5   Williams, *The Merthyr Rising*, pp.113–15

6   Jones, D, p.145

7   *The Cambrian*, 16 July 1831

8   *The Cambrian*, 16 July 1831; 23 July 1831

9   Isaac Evans, *Tarian y Gweithiwr*, 14 August 1884

10   Petition HO 17/128; Cordell, *Fire People*, p.370

11   *The Cambrian*, 18 June,1831

12   Petition, HO 17/128. Cordell, *Fire People*, pp.370–1

13   Isaac Evans, *Tarian y Gweithiwr*, 14 August 1884

CHAPTER 4: The Trial

1   Gatrell, V A C, *The Hanging Tree*, p.515

2   Gatrell, p.537

3   Henry Sockett came from Worcester, with links to Bath through his wife. He was admitted to Grays Inn in 1792, becoming a Bencher in 1821 and Treasurer in 1825. He was in Swansea by 1819, and was visitor at the Poorhouse there, where he was apparently regarded as firm but fair. He was given the freedom of the Borough of Swansea in 1830 and was registered as resident there until 1839. However, he seems to have divided his time between Swansea and London, where he was probably a stipendiary magistrate in Southwark until 1846. He was 66 years old at the time of the trial. There appear to be few, if any, records of his work as a barrister. Information from Neath Antiquarian Society.

4   Gatrell, p.534
5   Gatrell, p.539
6   The sources for the trial are *The Cambrian*, 15 and 22 July 1831; National Archives, HO 17/128, Part 2, bundle Zp; HO 41/28, Case 3; and a more modern article by Nicholas Cooke analysing the trial record and giving a lawyer's view of the proceedings, in T G Watkins, ed., *The Trial of Dic Penderyn and other essays.*
7   *The Cambrian*, 16 July 1831
8   *The Cambrian*, 23 July 1831
9   Price's second petition
10 Sekar, Satish, *The Cardiff Five*, p.182
11 *The Cambrian*, 23 July 1831

CHAPTER 5: Last Days

1   *The Cambrian*, 23 July 1831
2   Howells's diary
3   *The Cambrian*, 23 July 1831; *Merthyr Rising*, pp.184–5; Gatrell, pp.205, 617
4   Watkins, T G, *The Legal History of Wales*, Chapter 9
5   *The Cambrian*, 27 August 1831; Williams, *The Merthyr Rising*, p.193
6   Price, Watkin William, 'Joseph Tregelles Price', *Dictionary of Welsh Biography* (online). Information re Price's library from J V Hughes, formerly Local Studies librarian, West Glamorgan County Libraries.
7   *The Cambrian*, 6 August 1831
8   Isaac Evans, *Tarian y Gweithiwr*, 14 August 1884
9   *The Cambrian*, 6 August 1831
10 National Archives, HO 17/128; HO 52/16; HO 6/16; HO 13/58. Copies of some of the letters are in the Richard Burton Archives in Swansea University.
11 *The Cambrian*, 6 August 1831; execution data Gatrell, p.617
12 Islwyn ap Nicholas, p.55; information from Steffan ap Dafydd and John Morgan

13 *Y Drysorfa*, pp.418–19. Information on Dic's note from A L Evans and Allan Blethyn.

14, *Eurgrawn Wesleyaidd,* 1865 (pp.354–5) and 1870 (pp.355–6) (see Appendices)

15 *The Cambrian*, 20 August 1831

16 *Y Drysorfa*, pp.418–19

17 *Eurgrawn Wesleyaidd* 1865 and 1870 (see Appendices)

18 *The Cambrian*, 20 August 1831

19 J O'Brien, *Transactions of the Aberafan and Margam Historical Society*, 1934, p.118

Chapter 6: Aftermath

1 *The Cambrian,* 20 August 1831

2 *The Cambrian,* 27 August 1831

3 *The Cambrian,* 10 September 1831

4 *The Cambrian,* 17 September 1831

5 *The Cambrian,* 24 September 1831

6 Islwyn ap Nicholas; *Tarian y Gweithiwr,* 14 August 1884; *Y Drysorfa*

7 Glamorgan Archives, Cardiff, Q/S/R 1831 D. Quarter Session Rolls, 13 October 1831

8 *Rhondda Leader,* 2 June 1906; Jenkins, *All Against the Collar*

9 Williams, *The Merthyr Rising,* p.13

10 Thomas, G, *A Few Selected Exits,* pp.146–7

11 *Western Mail,* 23 March 1933

12 Press cutting dated 11 September 1964; the source is not noted, but is probably the *Port Talbot Guardian.*

13 Information from A L Evans

14 Information from Harri Webb

15 Information from Alan Jones

16 'Deathbed confession', *Tarian y Gweithiwr,* 31 July 1884

17 Isaac Evans, *Tarian y Gweithiwr,* 14 August 1884

18 For some reason Gwyn A Williams always thought it was the Church in Wales which was responsible for the present

monument, but though obviously the church authorities would have had to agree to the scheme, and now take part in the annual service, it was local trades unionists who organised it.

CHAPTER 7: Afterlife

1   Jones, Hefin, *Dic Dywyll y Baledwr*
2   Theatr Soar's performance of *My Land's Shore* was reviewed on p.25 of the *Western Mail*'s *Weekend* section, 24 February 2018
3   Thomas, G, *Plays and Players;* Thomas, G, *A Few Selected Exits,* pp.143–148
4   Information from Ian Meredith
5   Lewis, D Emrys, 'Was Dic Penderyn a Martyr?' in *Welsh Outlook*, Vol. xviii, August 1931, p.207
6   See Jones, S R, *Literary Tradition of the Neath and Afan Valleys* for background to Llewelyn

Picture Section

Dyffryn Barn, which Dic would have known, is shown on the right

A L Evans

Ironstone miners' cottages from Rhyd-y-car, now preserved at St Fagans National Museum of History

Lucas Migliorelli, CC BY 3.0/Wikimedia Commons

Revd Morgan Howells, Dic's brother-in-law
British School, public domain/Wikimedia Commons

High Street, Merthyr Tydfil, *c*.1850

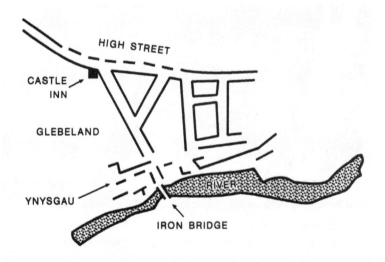

Dic's route away from the Castle Inn

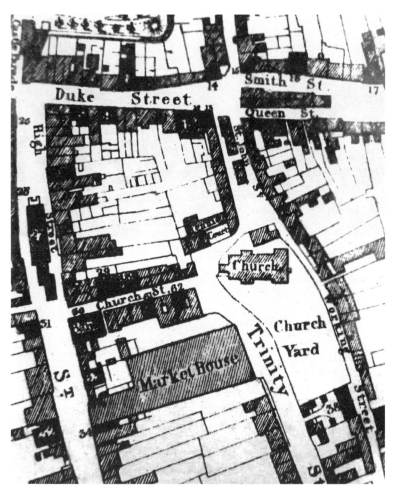

Central Cardiff in 1840, showing the site of the old gaol, now the Market, with Crockherbtown/Queen Street at the top of St John Street

John Wood's map of Cardiff, 1840. Cardiff Central Library

Revd Edmund Evans, who was with Dic at the execution

Old St Mary's Church, Aberafan, c.1850 – a much plainer, more countrified church with whitewashed walls and high-backed pews

The cross marking Dic's final resting place

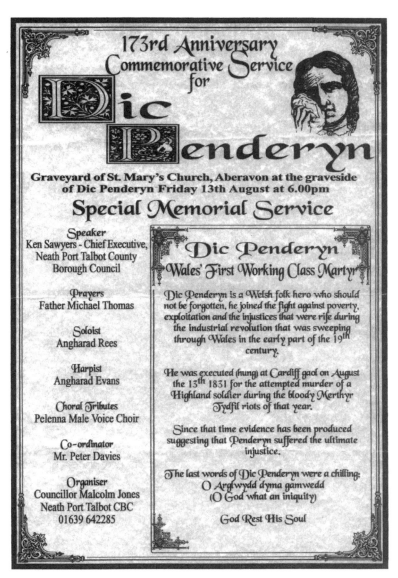

Programme from the annual memorial service commemorating Dic

Bibliography

CLIFFE, Charles Frederick, *The Book of South Wales, the Bristol Channel, Monmouthshire and the Wye* (Hamilton, Adams & Co, 1848 [Second Edition])

COOKE, Nicholas, 'The King versus Richard Lewis and Lewis Lewis' in T G Watkins, ed., *The Trial of Dic Penderyn and other essays* (University of Wales Press, 2003), pp.110–27

CORDELL, Alexander, *Requiem for a Patriot* (Weidenfeld & Nicolson, 1988), 352 pp.

CORDELL, Alexander, *The Fire People* (Hodder & Stoughton, 1972), 381 pp.

CRAIG, D and JONES, J, eds. *Cyfarthfa Chronicles* (Merthyr Writers Circle, 1993), 52 pp.

DAVIES, Lewis, *Ystoriau Siluria* (The Educational Publishing Co. Ltd., 1921), 150 pp., illus.

DONOVAN, Edward, *Descriptive Excursion through South Wales and Monmouthshire in the year 1804* (self-published/ Rivington, 1805), Vol. 2, pp.43–7

EDWARDS, Meinir Wyn, *Dic Penderyn* (Y Lolfa, 2008 [*Welsh Folk Tales* Series]), 24 pp., illus.

EVANS, Gwynfor, *Welsh Nation Builders* (Gomer Press, 1988)

EVANS, Isaac, *Tarian y Gweithiwr*, August 14 1884

GATRELL, V A C, *The Hanging Tree: Execution and the English People 1770–1868* (OUP, 1994), xx, 634 pp.

ISLWYN ap NICHOLAS, *Dic Penderyn: Welsh Rebel and Martyr* (Foyle's Welsh Press, 1945), 64 pp.

JENKINS, Clive, *All Against the Collar: Struggles of a White Collar Union Leader* (Methuen, 1990)

JONES, David, *Before Rebecca* (Allen Lane, 1973)

JONES, Hefin, *Dic Dywyll y Baledwr* (Gwasg Carreg Gwalch, 1995 [*Llyfrau Llafar Gwlad*]), 63 pp., illus.

JONES, Helen, 'The Search for Dic Penderyn' in *Glamorgan Family History Society*, March 1998

JONES, Sally Roberts, *Dic Penderyn: The man and the martyr* (Goldleaf Publishing, 1993), 20 pp.

JONES, Sally Roberts, *The Literary Tradition of the Neath and Afan Valleys, Maesteg and Porthcawl* (M.Phil. thesis, Swansea University, 2008)

LEWIS, D Emrys, 'A Forgotten Martyr' in *Transactions of the Aberafan and Margam Historical Society*, 1928, pp.8–9

LEWIS, D Emrys, 'Was Dic Penderyn a Martyr?' in *Welsh Outlook*, Vol. XVIII, No. 8, August 1931, pp.206–7

MATTHEWS, Edward, trans. and abridged by A L Evans, *Siencyn Penhydd and George Heycock*, (Port Talbot Historical Society, 1989), 100 pp.

MEREDITH, Ian, 'Dic Penderyn's Family – Alive and Well in Blaenrhondda!!!' in *Glamorgan Family History Society*, June 1998

MORGAN, E, *Boanerges, Neu Hanes Bywyd Parch. Morgan Howells* (privately printed, 1853)

MORGAN, Patrick and BUNKO, Anthony, *Dic Penderyn and the Merthyr Rising* (St David's Press, 2016 [*Tidy Tales from Welsh History*]), 118 pp., illus.

NICHOLAS, John, *Yr Hen Ddyffryn a Charmel a'u Canghenau* [sic] (T M Jones a'i Fab, Aberafan, n.d.)

O'BRIEN, J, 'Old St. Mary's Church, Aberavon' in *Transactions of the Aberavon and Margam Historical Society*, 1934, pp.114–31

ROBERTS, Gomer M, *Crogi Dic Penderyn* (Gwasg Gomer, 1977), 113 pp.

ROBERTS, Gomer, M, *Crwydro Blaenau Morgannwg* (Llyfrau'r Dryw, 1952)

SEKAR, Satish, *The Cardiff Five: Innocent beyond any doubt* (Waterside Press, 2012), 208 pp.

THOMAS, Gwyn, *A Few Selected Exits* (Seren Books, 1985), 212 pp.

THOMAS, Gwyn, *All Things Betray Thee* (Lawrence & Wishart, 1986), x,118 pp. (Second Edition, with introduction by Raymond Williams)

THOMAS, Gwyn, *Jackie the Jumper*, with an introduction by the author, in G Thomas, *Plays and Players*, February 1963, pp.25–44. The play was later published in Gwyn Thomas, *Three Plays* (Seren Books, 1990)

THOMAS, Hugh, gol., *Cyffro Cymdeithasol Yng Nghymru 1800–1843* (Gwasg Prifysgol Cymru, 1972 [*Cyfres Llygad y Ffynnon*]), 67 pp.

WATKINS, T G, *The Legal History of Wales* (University of Wales Press, 2007)

WEBB, Harri, *Dic Penderyn and the Merthyr Rising of 1831* (Penderyn Press, 1956)

WILIAM, Eurwyn, *Rhyd-y-Car: A Welsh mining community* (National Museum of Wales / D Brown and Sons, 1987) 28 pp., illus.

WILLIAMS, Gwyn A, 'Dic Penderyn: The making of a Welsh Working Class Martyr' in *Llafur: Journal of the Society for the study of Welsh Labour*, 2 *(3)*, September 1978, pp.110–22.

WILLIAMS, Gwyn A, 'The Merthyr of Dic Penderyn' in Glanmor Williams, ed., *Merthyr Politics: The Making of a Working Class Tradition* (University of Wales Press, 1966), pp.9–27

WILLIAMS, Gwyn A. *The Merthyr Rising* (Croom Helm, 1978), 237 pp.

WILLIAMS, John Stuart, *Dic Penderyn and other poems* (Gwasg Gomer, 1970), 64 pp.

WILLIAMS, Rhydwen, *The Angry Vineyard* (Christopher Davies, Swansea, 1972), 272 pp.

Newspapers and periodicals

Y Drysorfa, 1919, ixxxix, pp.418–19

The Cambrian, issues from July–August 1831

Eurgrawn Wesleyaidd, 1865, pp.354–5; 1870, pp.355–6

Y Fellten, 9 October 1874

Glamorgan Gazette, 17 March 1933

Rhondda Leader, 29 March 1990, p.3

Tarian y Gweithiwr, 31 July 1884; 14 August 1884

Western Mail, 14 October 1874; 30 March 1933; 19 May 1947

National Archives

HO 17/128, Part 2, bundle 7p

HO 41/28, Case 3

HO 52/16

HO 13/58

Index

Abbott, James 43, 50, 66–71,
74, 76–9, 83, 85–6, 90–2, 94,
105, 108, 120, 127, 135, 142,
156–9, 170

Aberafan 8, 10–11, 13–22, 27, 31,
84, 96, 98–100, 110–12, 114,
123, 128, 132, 134, 136, 139,
143, 152, 154–5, 161–3, 165–6

Abraham, David 57, 86

Abraham, William ('Mabon') 116

All Things Betray Thee 127–8,
133, 136–8, 140

Angharad's Isle 133–5, 137

Angry Vineyard, The 142–3

Black, Donald 56–7, 65–72, 74,
76–8, 80, 83, 91–3, 100, 102,
104, 107, 110, 112–13, 115,
120, 122, 132, 153, 156

Bosanquet, Mr Justice 59, 63–5,
72, 74, 76, 79–85, 87–90,
93–5, 106, 108, 117, 120–1,
143, 149

Brougham, Lord 87, 95

Bruce, J B (stipendiary
magistrate) 43, 46, 53, 55, 70

Cambrian, The 9, 46, 56, 62–3,
65, 67, 71–3, 79, 81, 87, 89,
95, 99, 100–2, 105–7, 117,
118, 121, 126, 136
response to the execution 101–4

Carmel Chapel, Aberafan 21–2,
24, 31, 84, 112, 169

Caroline, Queen 139

Castle Inn (/Castle Hotel) 38–9,
50–4, 56–7, 64, 66, 69–70,

73–5, 77, 83, 85–6, 90–3, 102,
104–6, 109, 115, 119, 124,
126–7, 134–5, 138, 140–1,
147, 158–60, 163, 171

Cato Street Conspiracy 40–1

chapels 14, 19–24, 32–4, 116,
142, 155

Coffin, Joseph 50, 86

Cooke, Nicholas 82, 114, 136,
172

Cordell, Alexander 9, 34, 122,
139–142

'Correspondent, A' 104–8

Corvice, Mary 62

Cound, Dafi 18, 19, 132, 162

Court of Requests 44–7, 50, 52,
116, 127, 134, 140, 141, 159

Crawshay, William 38, 42–6, 51,
53, 60, 64, 78, 129–30, 137,
142, 164

Crawshays, ironmasters 25, 28,
30

Darker, Thomas 70

David, William John 85, 91

Davies, Benjamin 57

Davies, David 62

Davies, Lewis 10–11, 19, 28,
112–14, 131–2, 136, 162–5,
169

Davies, Lucretia 62

Davies, Margaret 48, 50

'Dic Dywyll' 125–6, 142, 153

'Dic Penderyn' *passim*
childhood exploits 19–20
children 34–5
education 22–4

execution 96–9, 145–50
funeral 99, 132, 152–5, 165
last letter 165–7
marriage 34–5
nickname 15–16
trial 65–79
Dic Penderyn Society 123
Donovan, Edward 17–18
Drew, James 70, 76–7, 92
Dyffryn Barn, Taibach 15, 21–2

Edwards, Meinir Wyn 143
Edwards, William 92
Eurgrawn Wesleyaidd 9, 112, 145–9
Evans, Mr (junior prosecuting counsel) 68–71, 77
Evans, A Leslie 11, 112
Evans, Revd Edmund 96–7, 112, 145–50, 154
Evans, Elizabeth (daughter of Elizabeth and John Evans) 35, 110, 158, 170
family in the Rhondda 14, 35, 110, 170
Evans, Revd Evan, Nantyglo 113
Evans, Frederic, *see* Llewelyn, Michael Gareth
Evans, Isaac 10, 44, 49, 57, 79, 106, 109, 113, 120, 136, 155, 158–61, 166, 169
Evans, James 10, 13, 17, 33, 113, 122
Evans, John 35, 57, 105, 110, 122, 135, 141, 159, 166
Evans, Nancy (and son) 56–7

Fire People, The 9, 123, 139–41
Fothergills, ironmasters 24, 46
Frost, John 34, 122
funeral procession 98–100, 109, 111, 132, 139, 152–4

Gale, Charlie 14, 123–4
Griffiths, Lisa Morfa 111
Guest, Josiah John 38, 40, 53, 55, 67–8, 117
Guests, ironmasters 25, 30–1

hangman (and difficulty in finding one) 94, 95, 98, 150
Hardinge, Judge 37, 79
Harries, Elizabeth 24, 34–5, 57, 95–6, 110, 113, 122, 158–9, 166, 170
Hastings, Chris 128
Highlanders Regiment (93rd) 51, 53–5, 65, 100, 163
Hill, Anthony 52, 55
Hill, Samuel 37–8
Hills, ironmasters 25
Hirwaun 49, 55, 114, 131–2, 153, 160, 163
Hope Chapel, Newport 33–4, 122
Howells, Elizabeth 11, 14, 17, 19, 24, 28, 32–3, 35, 96, 122, 170
Howells, Revd Morgan 13, 19, 33–5, 81, 95, 97–9, 108, 122, 130, 140–2, 150–2, 154, 170
Hughes, David 63–5

Iniquity/Camwedd 143
Islwyn ap Nicholas 10–11, 18–19, 114, 133, 137, 166, 169

Jackie the Jumper 128–31
Jenkins, Clive 15, 21, 112
Jenkins family, Aberafan 16, 155, 168
Jenkins, Joan 48, 72–3
Jenkins, Mary, *see* Lewis, Mary (Dic's mother)
Jenkins, Richard Hoare (High Sheriff) 98, 133
John, William 62

Johns / John Winford 56
Jones, Alan 112
Jones, Revd Daniel 82, 89, 97,
    109
Jones, David (Aberafan
    portreeve) 31
Jones, David ('Dai Solomon') 56
Jones, David (Assizes case
    – perhaps also Dai Solomon,
    but unclear) 63–4, 78
Jones, David (historian) 12, 41,
    46, 137, 170–1
Jones, Francis 62
Jones, Robert 65
Jones, Revd T 97, 146–9
Jones, William (witness) 78, 91
Jones, Revd William 83, 89
Joseph, Martyn 127

Kenfig Hill 13–14
Kirkhouse, Henry 64, 78

Lettsom, Samuel Fothergill 24
Lewis, D Emrys 10, 132–3, 166
Lewis family 13ff., 19, 28, 32
    Lewis, Elizabeth (Dic's sister),
        see Howells, Elizabeth
    Lewis, Elizabeth (Dic's wife),
        see Harries, Elizabeth
    Lewis, John (Dic's brother)
        11, 13–14, 17, 28, 111, 122,
        151, 153
    Lewis, Lewis (Dic's father)
        13, 16, 17, 28, 32, 151
    Lewis, Mary (Dic's daughter)
        35, 96
    Lewis, Mary (Dic's mother)
        13–14, 16–17, 28, 32, 168
    Lewis, Matthew (Dic's
        brother) 11, 17, 28, 32, 98,
        122
    Lewis, Pamela (descendant of
        John Lewis) 14, 122

Lewis, Richard, see 'Dic
    Penderyn'
Lewis, Richard (Dic's son) 34
Lewis, Sarah (Dic's sister), see
    Morgan, Sarah
Lewis, James (surgeon at Cardiff
    Gaol) 89, 104
Lewis, Lewis, see 'Lewsyn yr
    Heliwr'
Lewis, Phillip 96
Lewis, Ronald 128
Lewis, Thomas 46–7, 49, 56,
    63–5
'Lewsyn yr Heliwr' 7, 16, 32, 46,
    49, 50, 52–4, 56, 58–9, 61,
    63–72, 74–6, 78–83, 85–90,
    93–5, 99, 101, 104–5, 108,
    114, 119–21, 124, 127–8, 130,
    132–6, 138, 140, 142, 148–9,
    153, 157, 163–4
Llafur: The Welsh People's
    History Society 41, 124, 139
Llewelyn, Michael Gareth 41,
    133–5, 138–9
Llewellyn, Thomas 43–7, 52,
    63–4, 78, 128, 134, 170
Luke, James 37

'Man of Glamorgan, A' 106–7,
    109, 126, 136
Marsden, Mr 91
Matthews, Edward 91
Maule, William Henry (chief
    prosecution counsel) 60, 66,
    72, 77
Melbourne, Lord 62, 65, 78,
    81, 87– 91, 93, 95, 106, 108,
    114–7, 120–1, 143
memorials 10, 123, 128
Merthyr Tydfil passim
    c.1819 24ff.
    customs and culture 26–7
    housing and conditions 28– 30

iron industry 25
labour unrest 1800 35–8
labour unrest 1816 38–40
post-Rising response 100, 109
Meyrick, Willliam 39, 43, 61–2, 68, 77–9, 89, 91
Morgan, David 62
Morgan, Henry and William 81
Morgan, John (Assizes case) 50, 73
Morgan, John (Dic's brother-in-law) 122
Morgan, Mary 37
Morgan, Rhodri 124
Morgan, Sarah 11, 17, 28, 32, 98, 113, 122
Morla, William 28, 49, 160–1, 169
Morris, E G 166
My Land's Shore 128

oral tradition 9–10, 14–15, 23, 31, 57, 79, 81, 83, 98, 110–11, 114, 123, 126, 130, 132–3, 135, 137–8, 143–4

Pardoe, Gwenllian 65
Parker, Ieuan/Ianto 112, 153
Penderyn cottage 13, 15–7, 151
Penderyn, Dic, *see* 'Dic Penderyn'
Penderyn (village near Hirwaun) 15–6, 46, 56, 134, 153, 163
Peterloo Massacre 2, 50, 93, 115
Phelps, John 46–8, 55, 63, 73
Phillips, Martin 11, 166, 169
Phillips, Thomas 62
Plater, Alan 128
policing 49–50, 159
Powell, Revd Lewis 83, 89
Price, Joseph Tregelles 56, 74, 77–9, 81–2, 84–88, 90–95, 105–9, 114, 117, 119, 122, 126, 136, 148, 170, 172

Prince Regent Inn, Cardiff 98, 152
Pudner, Huw 127–8
Pugh, Viv 123
Pyle 13, 15–17, 21, 32, 99, 111, 140, 151–4

Rees, Alun 128
Rees, Dafydd 22, 24, 169
Rees, David 91
Reform Bill / Parliamentary reform 42–5, 47, 55, 60, 78, 115, 117, 139, 153
Reynolds, John 84
Rhyd-y-car 28–29, 160–1, 169
Rice, James and wife 91
Richards, Elizabeth, *see* Evans, Elizabeth
Riot Act 38–9, 52–3, 64, 66, 69
Robert, Thomas 20–1
Rowland, Thomas 62
Rowland, William 69–70
Rowlands, Revd W 97, 146, 148–9

'Shoni Crydd' 50, 57, 79, 85–8, 105, 120–1, 124, 127, 159, 161
Smith, Robert 84
Smith, Sydney 61, 75
Sockett, Henry (chief defence counsel) 60, 63–4, 67–69, 71–2, 74–6, 104, 171
Sparks, Captain 71
Stephens, James 43–4
Stevens, Meic 127
Stuart, Lord James Crichton 87, 90, 95
'Subscriber, A' 107–8

Taibach 17–21, 139–40, 162
Talbot, C R M 87, 95
Taliesin ap Iolo, *see* Williams, Taliesin

Tarian y Gweithiwr 10, 113, 156–61
Taylor, Philip 50
Thomas, Albert 111
Thomas, David ('Dai Llawhaearn') 63–5
Thomas, Revd E W 99–100
Thomas, Gwyn 41, 111, 127–30, 133, 136–9
Thomas, John, *see* 'Shoni Crydd'
Thomas, William (squire) 43, 64
trial procedure 59–61
Twyn y Waun 45, 55, 126, 140

unions 10, 15, 21, 40–2, 48, 116–19, 122–3, 140–1, 161, 174

Vaughan, Thomas 63–5

Watkins, John Lloyd Vaughan 43
Watkins, T G 82
Webb, Harri 2, 10–11, 112–13, 173
Western Mail 10, 111, 131, 166, 168, 174
Westminster Review 30
William IV 87, 98
Williams, Aaron 37, 121
Williams, David (Assizes case) 63–4
Williams, Professor David 168

Williams, Revd David 96–8, 112, 145–9
Williams, Gwyn A 2, 9, 11–12, 41, 52–3, 110, 114, 123–4, 131, 136–7, 141, 168, 170–1, 173
Williams, Jane 48
Williams, John Stuart 126–8
Williams, Rhydwen 142–3
Williams, Richard, *see* 'Dic Dywyll'
Williams, Taliesin 27, 81, 90, 93, 132, 136, 142
Williams, Thomas 47, 56
Williams, William (Assizes case 1) 62
Williams, William (Assizes case 2) 62
Williams, William (special constable) 69
Winford, John, *see* Johns
women, role of 21, 30, 39, 44, 46–8, 72, 160
Wood, Colonel Thomas, MP 43
Woods, Mr (Governor of Cardiff Gaol) 103–4

Y Drysorfa 10, 13, 96, 113, 150–3, 155, 166
Year of Revolutions 115
Ynysgau Chapel, Merthyr 34, 160

Also from Y Lolfa:

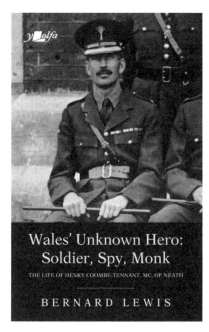

£12.99

Son of the Neath Coombe-Tennants, Henry's extraordinary life story includes a WWII POW-camp escape, parachuting into occupied France to assist the Resistance, and becoming a Benedictine monk.

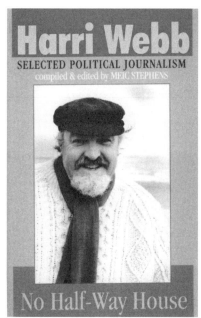

£9.95

A selection of the political writings of Harri Webb, which reflect both his Socialism and his Nationalism.